The Advent Tree

Visit **www.wjkbooks.com/AdventTree** to access free digital resources, which include group study session introduction videos from the author; worship resources that include liturgies, sermon suggestions, children's sermon scripts, prayers, and more; graphics to use in worship or group study; and coloring sheets of the images used in the book.

The Advent Tree

Meeting Jesus in God's Big Story

Kara Eidson

Illustrations by Kelli Cooper

First edition
Published by Westminster John Knox Press
Louisville, Kentucky

25 26 27 28 29 30 31 32 33 34—10 9 8 7 6 5 4 3 2 1

Book design by Drew Stevens
Cover design by Luisa Dias

Library of Congress Cataloging-in-Publication Data is on file at the Library of Congress, Washington, DC.

ISBN: 978-0-664-26931-9 (paperback)
ISBN: 978-1-646-98433-6 (ebook)

Printed in the United States of America

♾ The paper used in this publication meets the minimum requirements of the American National Standard for Information Sciences—Permanence of Paper for Printed Library Materials, ANSI Z39.48-1992.

For our husbands, Michael and Chris:
thank you for completing our family and joining us
in this amazing story!

—Kara and Kelli

Contents

Introduction

In the chaos leading up to Christmas, Christians enter into the season of Advent, a season of waiting and anticipation that extends four Sundays prior to December 25. The sacred season of Christmas extends from December 25 to January 5 (the "Twelve Days of Christmas" that we know so well from the popular holiday tune), ending with the celebration of Epiphany on January 6.

My Christmas tree goes up the weekend after American Thanksgiving, and I have packages wrapped and under the tree long before the holy days of Christmas begin. But in a globalized economy where we can have what we want almost as soon as we want it (think strawberries in January or free one-day shipping), the sacred call of anticipation may be more important than ever, especially for those who are preparing their hearts and minds for the coming of Christ during the season of Advent.

During my childhood, my family had a tradition of participating in a Jesse tree Bible study each December. As we counted down the days to Christmas, we read Scripture each day and added an embroidered symbol related to the Bible passage to the felt wall hanging my mother had made. My sister and I carefully kept track of whose turn it was to hang up each day's symbol and excitedly waited our turn. This is a treasured memory from my childhood, and I believe that this family tradition sparked my fascination with Scripture at an early age.

The Jesse for whom the tradition is named is the father of King David. The prophet Isaiah declared: "A shoot shall come out from the stump of Jesse, and a branch shall grow out of his roots" (11:1). At the time of this prophecy, the Northern Kingdom (Israel) had fallen to the Assyrians, and the Southern Kingdom (Judah) was about to fall to the Babylonians. In a time of profound hopelessness, Isaiah's prophecy offered assurance to the children of Abraham that God would send a leader from the lineage of the great King David who would restore Israel to its golden age and usher in an age of peace and justice. Christians traditionally see Jesus as this righteous leader, descended (as Matthew's genealogy says) from King David, and so this "stump of Jesse" has come to represent Jesus' connection to the Old Testament and all the events of Scripture prior to his actual birth.

Artistic renditions of the Jesse tree date as far back as the medieval period. The images can be found in many cathedrals, depicted in stained glass windows, tapestries, and a variety of other art forms, and were used to teach the stories of Scripture. I don't know at what point the Jesse tree became associated with Advent, but as a tradition for the time leading up to Jesus' birth, the Jesse tree has been used to explore the meaning of Jesus' birth in light of the full story of Scripture.

This book is an Advent study inspired by the tradition of the Jesse tree. We'll discover a family tree of Jesus that has roots in the Hebrew Scripture's stories of God and God's people passed down through the millennia and branches that extend beyond the people of Israel to include the whole world. Some of the stories we'll read are about people in Jesus' direct family lineage, but my focus is less on genealogy and more on answering the age-old question: "Who are we?" With that question in mind, I have chosen texts that tell the story of faith, from creation to the birth of Jesus Christ, in an exploration of the identity of the Christian people.

During the Christian season of Advent and the celebration of Christmas, we consistently come across language in Hebrew Scriptures that highlights the need for a savior. This language can be found in some of our most popular music, such as "O Come, O Come, Emmanuel" (Isa. 7:14) or the lyrics of Handel's *Messiah*: "For unto us, a child is born/unto us a Son is given . . ./and His name shall be called Wonderful,/Counsellor, the Mighty God,/ the Everlasting Father,/the Prince of Peace" (Isa. 9:6). While it is common to hear Hebrew Scriptures calling for a savior read during this season, these passages are often read out of their own historical and cultural context. Simultaneously, it is difficult to fully understand the significance of the birth of Jesus Christ without first understanding all that leads up to his birth.

The story of Jesus does not begin in Bethlehem over two thousand years ago. The story begins in Genesis with "in the beginning" (Gen. 1:1, RSV). The entirety of Hebrew Scripture influenced and informed the story of Jesus' life and ministry, and it also impacts how the Christian community views his death and resurrection. It is also vital to remember that the story of Jesus doesn't end with the ascension. The story of Jesus continues into our present and is the story of where we are headed in the future. This Advent and Christmas season, we will explore God's greater story of the past, how it can inform us in the present, and how that story carries us into the future.

HOW TO USE THIS BOOK

From the First Sunday of Advent through Epiphany on January 6, each day has a Scripture reading and accompanying devotional, followed by questions that can be used for discussion or for private reflection. Following the inspiration of the Jesse tree, each day's Scripture is paired with a symbol. Illustrations of each symbol can serve several purposes:

You can use the symbols included in the book as a form of *visio divina*, a monastic practice. Adapted from the practice of *lectio divina*, in which one reads a passage of Scripture repeatedly and meditates on it, participants in *visio divina* are encouraged to choose a religious image and then look at the image, meditate on its meaning, pray about the image, and spend time in contemplation simply resting in God's presence.

If you enjoy having something to do with your hands while reflecting, you can download coloring pages with the symbol for each day at www.wjkbooks.com/AdventTree. There are more complex versions for adults and simplified coloring pages for kids. For those using this study, whether as an individual or family, I encourage you to think of your coloring time each day as a spiritual practice. Consider reading the Scripture and the day's devotional first, and then spend time in reflection and prayer on the readings while you color. Coloring each page can be used as a time of meditation during the Advent season. Find a place in your home to display your coloring pages throughout the season. While many of us no longer display our artwork on the refrigerator in our adult years, it's beautiful to see the story unfold before your eyes as you approach Christmas day and then move through the days leading to Epiphany.

If you are using this study as a congregation or in a small group, you might consider creating a large Christmas tree out of green butcher block paper somewhere within the church building. As the tree fills with the symbols and creative works of the congregation, it will be a fun way to see how people are participating at home.

There are twelve family devotions included in this book, with devotionals geared toward families with kids who are preschool and elementary aged. These family devotions follow the general arc of the daily devotions included in the book but are age appropriate for younger participants. These include a simplified illustration for each of the twelve devotions, discussion questions, and a repeat-after-me-prayer for the entire household.

Also available online are resources for pastors and worship leaders to use *The Advent Tree* as their worship series during the Advent/Christmas seasons. The downloadable worship resources packet includes liturgical resources, community questions, prompts for children's time and repeat-after-me prayers, suggestions for worship art, and sermon prompts for each Sunday and holy day. All direct quotations of scripture are from the NRSVue.

Advent Week One

The Stump of Jesse

When Tolkien wrote The Lord of the Rings, he wrote it as one complete book. His publisher was appalled at the length of the book, insisting no one would ever buy a book that long. Tolkien publicly disliked his publisher's final decision to break up the lengthy story into three separate books. However, any LOTR devotee can tell you that all three books are critical for understanding the long and complicated story.

There are a multitude of characters and stories present throughout the text that Christians include as canon in the book we call the Bible. Sometimes it's hard to follow and keep up. While the books included in the Christian Bible were written by many authors across the span of centuries, our body of sacred text is comprised of different ways and extensions of telling the story of God and God's people. Although our Bibles divide the Hebrew Scriptures—the Old Testament—from the books of the New Testament, the Christian tradition upholds that they are part of the same story. As Isaiah's stump of Jesse metaphor suggests, new shoots have old roots. We cannot understand the birth of Jesus Christ, including its historical, spiritual, and cultural significance, without understanding the greater story into which this birth takes place. Our Christian story does not begin on Christmas Day; it begins in the dark void in the first chapter of Genesis.

Through Advent, we will explore various parts of this story, constantly asking the questions: (1) Who is God? (2) Who are we as God's people? and (3) How does God call us to be in community with the Divine, one another, and the entirety of God's creation? It would be hubris to assume we will find all the answers—but I believe the beauty of faith is in the journey, in asking the questions, in exploring the answers. As we prepare for and anticipate the coming of Christ, we will try to further understand how Jesus fits into God's greater story, in the hopes of better understanding how each of us fit into God's greater story as well. Just as Tolkien believed The Lord of the Rings belonged within one book because it is the same story, all the different stories of the Bible combine to tell us one great story about the Divine.

SUNDAY

A Branch of the Tree of Jesse
Isaiah 11:1–9

Throughout the Hebrew Scriptures, the reign of King David is often remembered as a golden age for Israel. This is why Isaiah invoked David—via David's father, Jesse—when prophesying hope to the people of Israel, saying "A shoot shall come out from the stump of Jesse, and a branch shall grow out of his roots" (v. 1).

After the exodus of the Hebrew people from Egypt, they settled in the land of Israel where judges initially ruled the nation, but eventually the rule was turned over to King Saul. After Saul's death, David was crowned the next king. After the death of David's son Solomon, Israel split into the Northern Kingdom (Israel) and the Southern Kingdom (Judah). At the time of the prophecy in today's text, the people of Judah watched nervously as Israel was defeated by the Assyrian Empire. The Assyrians posed a constant threat on Judah's northern border. When Babylon rose against their Assyrian occupiers, the Assyrian Empire transformed into the Babylonian Empire, which would eventually conquer Judah.

Isaiah uses the stump metaphor to compare the fall of Israel and Judah to the felling of Jesse's family tree. To fully understand this metaphor, it's important to know that when trees are chopped down, many species will set off shoots from the stump and begin to grow again; as long as the roots are viable, there is still hope that the tree might live. Isaiah promises the people of Judah that the roots of Yahweh's people are still strong, despite everything they might see in the moment. In a time of profound hopelessness, Isaiah's prophecy offered assurance to the children of Abraham that God would send a leader from the lineage of King David who would be as powerful as King David and who would usher in an age of peace and justice.

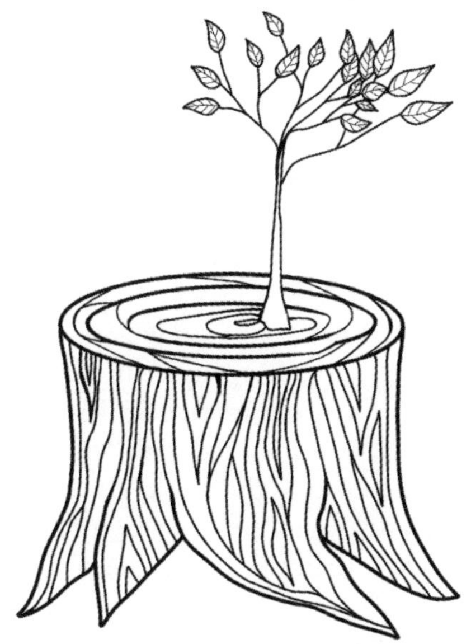

Isaiah's prophecy assures its readers of a future peace so complete that not only will war cease to exist but also nature itself will live in peace and harmony: "The wolf shall live with the lamb; the leopard shall lie down with the kid; the calf and the lion will feed together, and a little child shall lead them" (v. 6).

The Gospel writers of both Matthew and Luke carefully include King David as one of Jesus' ancestors when they list his family tree. Both wrote that Jesus was the fulfillment of the long-promised and long-awaited Messiah and develop their cases by invoking prophecies like today's reading. In the Hebrew Scriptures, we repeatedly read that this promised peace will arrive with the coming Messiah.

While this idyllic future has yet to come to fruition, we long, like our forebearers, for the just and peaceful world promised by Isaiah. In the season of Advent, Christians prepare for the coming of Christ in the past, present, and future. We prepare for the coming of Christ in the past by preparing to celebrate the birth of Jesus Christ in Bethlehem. The coming of Christ in the present depends on those who seek to follow Jesus as we attempt to live into the powerful words of the Lord's Prayer: "thy Kingdom come, thy will be done, on earth as it is in heaven." We invite Christ to join us in the present by working in the here and now to create this peaceable kin-dom promised by the long line of prophets. Finally, we look forward to the future coming of Christ, a time when peace will reign in God's new kin-dom.

As we move toward the hope of Christmas—God with us—we remember that even when it seems all is lost, hope (including hope for peace) is still alive when the roots are strong. In John 14:27, Jesus assures his disciples, "Peace I leave with you; my peace I give to you. I do not give to you as the world gives. Do not let your hearts be troubled, and do not let them be afraid." Through this Advent, we will explore how God has been with humankind in the past and present and how God promises to be part of our story in the future. Through our study of texts, prayerful discernment of their historical context, and application in our modern lives, we will strengthen our roots as people of faith and expand our understanding of the hope Christmas brings.

1. Today's symbol is a tree stump. What does the symbol mean in the context of today's Scripture reading?

2. What stands out to you in Isaiah's poetic prophecy? Which lines resonate with you most deeply and why?

3. In the season of Advent, we prepare for the coming of Christ in the past, present, and future. How does this passage inform us of the past for God's people and what the future may hold?

MONDAY

Birth of Isaac
Genesis 18:1–15; 21:1–7

God promised Abraham and Sarah that if they followed God's commands and entered into covenant with God, the Divine would make a great nation of their descendants. Because of this promise, Abraham and Sarah were expecting to have children, but many years passed, and Sarah had yet to conceive and give birth to a child.

In the ancient Near East, the predominant cultural understanding was that a woman's purpose was to bear sons for her husband. Because this was a strictly patriarchal society, women had very little agency within the culture, and having sons was one way to gain a sense of agency during that era. By this stage in her life, Sarah had reached an age where she was considered barren or unable to have children. The assumption was, in a world without birth control, that a fertile woman would get pregnant if she was in a marital relationship. True to their patriarchal culture,

there was no consideration that a fertility issue might stem from the male. In the context of today's Scripture, infertility caused a woman like Sarah to feel as if she was failing to live into her God-given purpose.

It is entirely possible that Sarah's "old age" may have actually been thirty years, or even twenty-five. Why, then, does the text say she was ninety years old? Have you ever heard someone tell a fishing story where the fish starts out the size of a goldfish, but after telling the story multiple times, the fish has become the size of a shark? Keep in mind that Sarah's story was shared by oral tradition for hundreds of years before being written down and was not intended to be taken literally. Today, we believe history should consist of precise and accurate facts. In that time, sharing oral history was not intended as a precise accounting of the fact but was instead used to convey an important message or truth.

When God's messengers appeared to Abraham by the oak trees and told him that Sarah would finally conceive, Sarah, who overheard, laughed with amused skepticism, an attitude of: "How can this be?" Sarah's amusement at the proclamation eventually led to how she named her son: the Hebrew word *laugh* (*tsachaq*) is wordplay into the name Isaac (*Yitschaq*), which means "he laughs."

God is faithful to the covenant made with Sarah and Abraham, and their descendants turned out to be more numerous than the stars in the sky. But while we know the end of the story, in the moment of today's Scripture, Sarah does not. Sarah's shock and disbelief are understandable. She carried the heavy weight of infertility while waiting many years for this moment to come to pass.

There are seasons in all our lives when it is difficult to believe good will happen again. There are times when it feels as though nothing good could possibly be a part of our future stories. During my time as a campus minister, when I provided pastoral care to young adults in the midst of rapid changes in their lives, I observed that they often experienced each traumatic event as endless. When I transitioned back into the local church, I was reminded that these overwhelming moments, and the panic we feel at a loss of control, are not confined to the realms of youth. At all ages, sometimes the circumstances of life hit us so hard and so repeatedly that we are convinced that this horrible time will last forever.

As we reflect on the birth of the baby Isaac, we also continue to look forward to the birth of Jesus, the physical embodiment of "God with us." We are called to remember that God never abandons us, and God never leaves us. God has promised to be with us in all times and places, even the worst that this life has to offer. God wanted to be with us so much that God came incarnate to live among us. God can be a companion for us, even in times of hopelessness. God is always a part of our story.

1. Today's symbol is an oak tree. What does the symbol mean in the context of today's Scripture reading?

2. Have you ever received news that you felt was too good to be true? Have you ever received news that made you laugh because the possibility that it might be true was so outrageous? What was the news, and what were the circumstances?

3. Name a season in your life when it felt like nothing could go right. What were the circumstances? How did you feel? Did you feel God's presence with you in that difficult time? If so, is that what kept you going? If not, what kept you holding on to your faith in God's goodness?

TUESDAY

Jacob Becomes Israel

Genesis 28:10–18; 32:24–32

Abraham and Sarah had their son, Isaac, who grew up and married Rebekah. Isaac and Rebekah had two sons, Jacob and Esau. Jacob and Esau were twins, and even their birth was a foreshadowing of their future struggles; Jacob followed Esau out of the womb by grasping Esau's ankle. The name Jacob even translates to "heel-grabber." In their culture, the lion's share of inheritance went to the firstborn male, so the symbolism of their birth story is that Jacob entered the world attempting to usurp his older brother to gain this bulk of the inheritance. Clearly his attempt as a newborn failed, but through two incidents in young adulthood, Jacob did manage to trick his way into claiming Esau's birthright and inheritance (see Gen. 25:21–34 and 27:1–38). Esau was so angry that he threatened to kill his brother, and Jacob fled for fear of his life.

Today's reading includes two stories in which Jacob received reassurance of God's presence with him, despite all that had happened. When Jacob was first on the run, one night he had a dream about God speaking to him and a vision of a ladder ascending into heaven. When he woke up in the morning, he set up an ebenezer to mark the site as holy (Gen. 28:18). An ebenezer, literally meaning "stone of help," is a way of marking a particularly holy place by setting up a large stone or pile of stones.

Years later, Jacob finally decided to apologize to Esau, and his brother agreed to meet to attempt reconciliation. Jacob was distraught and nervous as he prepared to meet with Esau, waiting for this long-anticipated meeting. It is during this night of sleepless anticipation that Jacob saw a stranger whom he determined must be a messenger from God, and they wrestled until daybreak. This divine encounter was memorialized not by God setting up a rock but by God renaming Jacob. The messenger gave Jacob a blessing and a new name: Israel, which means "one who struggles with God." Jacob named the holy place where he had wrestled with God Peniel, meaning, "I have seen God face-to-face, yet my life is preserved."

Throughout the Bible, we frequently encounter the importance of names and renaming, from Abram to Abraham, Sarai to Sarah, Jacob to Israel, Simon to Peter, and Saul to Paul. God gives great significance to names and to naming. Jacob demanded a blessing and was renamed "one who struggles with God." At first glance, it might seem strange that a divine being would want followers who struggle with their god, but this tells us a lot about Yahweh, the God of Israel. Often a lack of faith or feeling separated from God brings us great shame. But I would offer a reframing of struggling with our faith: the Divine delights when we struggle with God, simply because this struggle means we still have faith. We see throughout the Gospels that Jesus, who's arrival we anticipate as we prepare for Christmas, most frequently taught through stories, metaphors, and questions. Indeed, the story of God's people consistently comes back, time and time again, to those who wrestle with questions of God. But even in wrestling, they are deemed faithful. In Mary Doria Russell's novel *The Sparrow*, a priest speaks these words at the funeral of a beloved friend: "The Jewish sages also tell us that God dances when His children defeat Him in argument, when they stand on their feet and use their minds. So questions . . . are worth asking. To ask them is a very fine kind of human behavior. If we keep demanding that God yield up answers, perhaps someday we will understand them. And then we will be something more than clever apes, and we shall dance with God."[1]

1. Today's symbol is an ebenezer. What does the symbol mean in the context of today's Scripture reading?

2. How did you receive your name? What does your name mean? If you don't know the answers to these questions, do some research with family or online. What is the significance of your name to you?

3. What does it signify that Israel means "one who struggles with God"? Does this information bring you comfort in your own spiritual journey? Why or why not?

WEDNESDAY

Joseph and His Brothers
Genesis 42:1–8; 45:1–20

Today's Scripture contains so much family drama between Jacob and his sons that it could easily be mistaken for a soap opera if we set the story in modern times. We are reading only a small portion of the story today, but some summary of the full story is necessary to appreciate today's text in context.

After Jacob fled from home when Esau threatened his life, he fell in love with his cousin Rachel but was tricked into marrying Rachel's sister Leah before he could eventually marry Rachel as well. Leah had seven sons and had her maid Zilpah bear two sons on her behalf. Rachel had her maid Bilhah bear two sons on her behalf. After a lengthy stretch of infertility, the beloved Rachel finally gave birth to a son, Joseph, who became Jacob's favorite among his twelve sons. In a great display of this favor, Jacob gave Joseph a very special "ornamented robe" (Gen. 37:23).

Many of us grew up hearing about Joseph's coat of many colors, and there is even an entire Broadway musical named after

Joseph's coat. As much as I hate to disappoint fans of musical theater, "coat of many colors" is actually a Greek mistranslation perpetuated in English by the King James Bible. The original Hebrew description is a little vague, but the point is that the garment marks Joseph as special and set apart from his brothers.

Joseph understands his special standing and lords his status over his jealous brothers. They eventually sell him into slavery and convince their father that Jacob died while tending the sheep. Joseph rose in the ranks during his time in Egypt, eventually becoming the top adviser to the pharaoh. Joseph correctly interpreted a dream of the pharaoh that predicted seven years of abundance followed by seven years of famine, and he was put in charge of collecting surplus from the years of plenty to prepare for the years of famine.

When the famine in the region hit Jacob's family, they heard there was food to spare in Egypt, so they traveled there to beg for assistance. The brothers did not recognize Joseph as the distributor of the food in Egypt when they arrived and asked for grain—and although Joseph put them through a complex set of misdirection, in the end, he agreed to help his family. See what I mean about this story sounding like a soap opera?

Although technology has transformed our world into one that would be unrecognizable to the people of the ancient world, I suspect they would easily recognize the sins we commit in modernity. Like the people of Joseph's time, we still struggle in our own era with similar character flaws to the ones we find in this ancient soap opera: jealousy, greed, hatred, and the desire for revenge are still rampant among us.

Perhaps the most important takeaway from this story is that God remains Joseph's constant companion. As we continue our journey to the manger in Bethlehem, we see how God was always a part of Joseph's story, even in times of devastation and hopelessness. Despite Joseph's brothers' worst intentions, God was able to turn their actions into good that continued to fulfill the covenant made with Abraham and Sarah. The God who created the cosmos can surely create something worth salvaging, even when we are in crisis and unable to see God's hand at work within our stories. Just as God did not abandon Joseph, even when he was cast down into a literal pit of despair, God will not abandon us.

1. Today's symbol is a bag of grain. What does the symbol mean in the context of today's Scripture reading?

2. Name a time when you have experienced drama within your own family. Although sometimes family members must be cut out of our lives for our own health, forgiveness is still an essential part of the healing process. Have you healed from that family drama, or are you still working on healing and forgiveness?

3. God is not the one who sells Joseph into slavery in Egypt; this is an evil that his brothers commit. But God is able to work through something so horrible to create something beautiful for the children of Israel. How might God be able to work in your own life to turn something painful into something beautiful that can be used for the greater glory of God?

THURSDAY

Time of the Judges
Judges 2:11–21

God's people remained in Egypt after the time of Joseph. Eventually a pharaoh rose who did not recall Joseph, and the Hebrew people became enslaved. After a time, God called Moses to lead the Hebrew people out of slavery in Egypt, and Joshua was the clear successor following Moses' death. After Joshua's death, there was a power vacuum, and without clear leadership, the people struggled. At this point, God decided that the people would be ruled over by judges—wise people who helped decide what actions to take, how to keep people safe, and how to solve disputes among the people. Frequently the judges were also military rulers.

In the text today, we read that the people of Israel turned away from Yahweh and began to worship other gods, including Baal and Astarte. In ancient semitic languages, *ba'al* meant "lord or ruler" and eventually became a word that was used as a name for several gods in the pantheons of the region. There were multiple forms of Baal portrayed across the ancient Near East, and while this text does not give us enough specifics to determine which form of Baal it is referencing, it is likely the god worshiped by the Canaanite people. The Baal of the Canaanites was associated with fertility, crops, and weather (specifically as the bringer of rains). In a primarily agrarian society, it is not difficult to understand why the god of crops and fertility was highly praised throughout the region.

Astarte was a god who was common in the pantheons of that region, although in other places she was known as Ishtar, and in at least one culture, the two names were used interchangeably. She was most frequently revered as the goddess of war and/or sexuality. In an agrarian culture frequently at war with their neighbors, it is not difficult to understand the appeal of such a deity.

While today's text states that the people worshiped Baal and Astarte specifically, it is possible that the names used for the other gods are simply generic stand-ins to indicate that the people turned away from Yahweh and began to practice the pagan faiths that were common in the region.

Today's Scripture passage from Judges succinctly outlines a consistent pattern that we find throughout Hebrew Scriptures. There is a constant cycle at play: (1) God makes covenant with the people, (2) the people are faithful, and good things happen, (3) the people drift away from God, and bad things happen when God brings about some sort of divine judgement, and (4) the people repent, and God forgives them, taking them back. If you read the Hebrew Scriptures long enough, you might frequently find yourself repeating the phrase: "same song, different verse." It's like watching the movie *Groundhog Day*—the circumstances around the day may change, but it keeps repeating itself.

I suspect this cycle is all too familiar to most people of faith. Although we might not turn and worship other deities, a consistent cycle of feeling close to God, followed by a time of feeling far away from God, is something we can all recognize. Most of us have lived a similar cycle in our own spiritual lives. We may call the gods of our modern world by other names, but the parts of life that draw us away from God—which we call sin—are abundant, alive, and well. What does it mean for us to consistently turn back toward God?

This is the purpose of Advent, a time for contemplating how we might turn toward God as a way to prepare for the coming of God incarnate. In many ways, capitalism has co-opted the sacred season of Advent. We are carefully instructed by commercials to celebrate the Christmas season by purchasing a whole bunch of stuff: toys, presents, food, drink, etc. The gods of wealth, greed, and indulgence are alive and well—and all too alluring—during this time of the year. I confess that, most days in December, I would rather spend time wrapping fun Christmas gifts than contemplating divine truth. After Thanksgiving celebrations have concluded, I would rather blissfully bask in the lights on my Christmas tree than contemplate my own sin. And this is why it is so critical that as Christian people, we pause during this season of celebrations of material abundance to consider how we are turning our attention to the Divine and how God is at work within the stories of our lives.

1. Today's symbol is a set of justice scales. What does the symbol mean in the context of today's Scripture reading?

2. What gods attract the people of our modern world? What are some of the things that draw you away from God?

3. How do you find your way back to a path that is faithful? How do you repent—turn around—and come back into right alignment with the Divine?

FRIDAY

Samuel Anoints David
1 Samuel 16:1–13

While the judges ruled over Israel, they ran the nation as a theocracy, with the judges collaboratively in positions of human authority. The people began to look around and see that all the other nations around them had a king, and like teenagers longing for the latest fashion or fad, they decided they should also have a king. The people came to God over and over again, asking God to give them a king. God repeatedly insisted that a king was a bad idea, as one person with ultimate power can be easily corrupted or led astray. But the people kept insisting they needed a king.

After some time, God gave the people what they asked for and made Saul the first king of Israel. Unfortunately, as Saul's reign wore on, he became increasingly paranoid. Saul suffered from physical and mental afflictions, including severe delusions. As Saul became emotionally unstable, his reign became increasingly politically unstable. Eventually, God called the prophet Samuel to anoint a new king outside of Saul's bloodline. This act—if discovered by Saul or any of his supporters—could have been classified as treason, a crime punishable by death.

David's anointing is a shocking moment in the historical context of today's Scripture reading. In the social context of that time, birth order held enormous significance. Since David was the youngest among many brothers, his father did not even think to bring him in from the fields when he was asked to present his sons. Even Samuel was shocked when God chose David, as Samuel had expected one of the older and more impressive brothers to be the one he had come to anoint. The act of anointing David is shocking because lineage is at the very foundation of a monarchy—and David was not related to Saul by any bloodlines. Finally, David seemed a surprising choice because kings of that era led their troops into battle when the nation went to war. David was still a child and was not someone who would inspire confidence among fully grown men headed into battle. Simply put: David did not make sense as a candidate for the next king of Israel.

Yet David was the one God chose—and so Samuel anointed him with oil. This act of anointing meant that the anointed would be set apart for a special purpose. The act of anointing was seen as a holy seal in which scented olive oil was poured over the head and face of the anointed. Olive oil was an extremely valuable substance in the ancient world, as thousands of olives are required to produce one meager liter of olive oil.

The word *messiah* literally means "anointed one." As Christians living through the season of Advent, we look forward to the arrival of the one we hail as the Messiah in the birth of Jesus Christ. In the same way that God chose David, the least likely in his family, to become the next king of Israel, God sent Jesus, who did not live into many of the expectations, to be the long-prophesied Messiah. By the time Jesus entered the world, the Jewish community of his time was expecting the Messiah to be a great military leader who would overthrow and expel the Roman Empire from the nation of Israel. Instead of living into human expectations, carrying a sword, and leading armies, Jesus came with teachings of love and grace, encouraging those who wanted to follow him to love God and love their neighbor.

In many ways, Christians fail to see our own worth in how we may be called or chosen by God. Our culture trains us to focus on our flaws and weaknesses and overlook the divine light within each of us. In the same way David was chosen, we must prayerfully discern how God calls each of us and how we might live out our faith in unexpected ways. As we continue to grow closer to the coming of Christ on Christmas Day, may we continue to ask how we can grow closer to this God of the unexpected.

1. Today's symbol is an oil flask. What does the symbol mean in the context of today's Scripture reading?

2. Describe a time when you made a negative judgment about a person and then they pleasantly surprised you. How might the Holy Spirit have been at work through this experience?

3. Why was Samuel so unnerved by what God had called him to do? Has God ever called you to do something that you didn't expect? How do you find the courage to do brave things when God calls you?

SATURDAY

Build Houses and Plant Gardens
Jeremiah 29:5–14

After the death of King David, his son Solomon took the throne and built the temple in Jerusalem. After the reign of King Solomon, however, the nation of Israel was divided into two separate nations: Israel to the north and Judah to the south. The Northern Kingdom was conquered by the Assyrians in 722 BCE, and the Southern Kingdom was eventually conquered by the Babylonians around 587 BCE. The Babylonian Empire sent the best and brightest people of their newly conquered territory back into the center of Babylon. This meant that anyone with the power, intelligence, or skill to lead an uprising was involuntarily moved out of Judah and into the heart of Babylon.

In the ancient world, many cultures shared a common belief that their god or gods accompanied them into battle. Therefore, when one army conquered another army, the prevailing belief was that the winning army must have the stronger god or gods. When Judah fell to Babylon, the people were convinced not only that their army had failed but also that the God of Abraham had failed. They had to struggle with this on a theological level and grapple with what it meant to be the children of Yahweh if Yahweh could lose.

Furthermore, up until this time, the Jewish people believed Yahweh could be worshiped only in the temple in Jerusalem. Suddenly, they did not have the choice to travel to Jerusalem, because the temple had been destroyed. Fundamental tenets of their faith had been undermined, and they had to rebuild their spiritual lives in the midst of the other trauma and loss they suffered.

The people of Judah living in Babylonian exile initially expected that they would be returning home quite soon—surely their rescue by Yahweh was imminent! They found it incredibly difficult and painful to receive Jeremiah's message that boiled down to, "You are going to be in exile for a long time. Settle down, build houses, plant gardens, because this is not a temporary situation." No one takes the time to build a house or plant a garden when they know their living status in that location is temporary.

Jeremiah promised the people that God was still with them, still heard their cries, and wanted them to live fully, even in the midst of exile. God wanted them to invest in their futures, even though the exile would be much longer than the people had hoped for. God wanted the people to remember that even in the most difficult of circumstances, hope abides.

As Christians, we find our ultimate hope through the life, teachings, sacrifice, and resurrection of Jesus Christ. As the days grow shorter and colder and as nights last longer and longer, the dead of winter is not a season associated with the hope that comes with growth and new life. But in the midst of this barren season, Christians celebrate the arrival of our ultimate hope, nearly coinciding with the longest night of the year (around December 21) in the northern hemisphere. In one of my favorite *Dr. Who* episodes, one character defines it in this way: "On every world, wherever people are, in the deepest part of the winter, at the exact midpoint, everybody stops, and turns, and hugs, as if to say 'Well done. Well done, everyone! We're halfway out of the dark.' Back on Earth, we called this Christmas."[2]

The winter solstice is the turning point after which the sun's light will last a little longer each day. Although Jeremiah delivers the news that the exile will last longer, it also comes with a message of hope that it will not be forever. As Christians, we know that even though God's kin-dom has not yet arrived, the life of Jesus means we, also, are halfway out of the dark.

1. Today's symbol is a garden. What does the symbol mean in the context of today's Scripture reading?

2. Have you ever believed yourself to be in a lousy—but temporary—situation that turned out to be not so temporary? What happened when you had to come to terms with your new reality? How can faith support us when we encounter these crossroads in life?

3. Have you ever reconsidered something that you used to believe? (This doesn't have to be faith related.) What changed your mind? How did it influence the way you live out your life? How did it change the way you live out your faith?

Advent Week Two
A People Seeking God

Throughout Scripture, God and God's people have been in a constant relationship. We see this relationship at work even in the story of creation. However, as soon as God's work of creation is complete, human beings begin repeatedly falling away from God, an archetype that remains powerful through the rest of Scripture. But even when God's people turn away, God's love remains steadfast.

God establishes a covenant with Abraham and Sarah, and they become the ancestors of the Hebrew, Israelite, and eventually Jewish people. A covenant is more than a simple pinkie promise made on the playground. A covenant is similar to a legal contract but is specifically made between the Divine and human beings. Time and time again, God's people fail to live up to their end of the covenant. Through the stories found in Hebrew Scripture, we find this repeated pattern of God's people falling in and out of love with the Divine.

Understanding the covenant God made with Abraham and Sarah helps us understand the greater tapestry of the story into which Jesus is born. As a Jew, Jesus would have learned from childhood this history of his people's journey with God.

Christians believe that Jesus Christ represents a new covenant with God's people without abolishing the original covenant with our Jewish siblings (see Matt. 5:17). We believe that this new covenant is representative of God's everlasting grace.

Throughout both covenants, humankind's relationships with God ebbs and flows; sometimes the people are close to God, and sometimes the people move away. In the same way, individual believers have and will fall into this same pattern—something many of us may even recognize through the narrative of our own lives. This week we will explore stories of how individuals' and all of Israel's relationship with God ebbed and flowed, and we will see how this back-and-forth story leads us to the manger and, finally, to our own stories with God.

SUNDAY

Prince of Peace
Isaiah 9:2–7

On Halloween, it is common practice for neighborhood residents to turn on their porch lights to indicate they are receiving trick-or-treaters. When we are expecting someone to arrive after dark, my husband and I turn on the porch light to light the way. We use light not only for safety but also to welcome people. Today's reading from Isaiah uses this common theme of a light showing the way through the darkness of a time when the people felt distant from God.

Isaiah 9 was written after the fall of Israel but before the fall of Judah. The king of Judah had repeatedly violated the covenant with Yahweh, putting trust in the powers of this world rather than the power of God. The people of Judah had turned away from God—the temple was stripped of its gold, which was given in homage to Assyria and their gods. Although they had sold out Israel to the Assyrian Empire, the people of the Southern Kingdom still lived in terror of the Assyrians, who loomed over them, consistently trying to beat back their northern borders—even though Judah was eventually conquered by the Babylonian Empire.

This ebb away from the Divine resulted in a particularly dark time for the people of Judah. Today's Scripture passage looked ahead to a time when the Assyrian threat would no longer hang over them and a new period of peace would begin. Isaiah prophesies of a time when the pendulum will swing back toward the people living faithfully into their covenant with God, predicting that a time of peace would be the result. Some scholars have even suggested that this passage is actually a coronation hymn for a king who was to come.

Many of us may recognize words from this passage, as they are used in the well-known lyrics of Handel's *Messiah*. Although the people of Judah were the original intended audience for this text, it has been frequently interpreted through the Christian lens to be addressing the coming of Jesus as the Messiah.

Regardless of which lens we use to read this text, at its heart is a promise that something better is on its way, and there is every reason to keep hope alive. "The people who walked in darkness have seen a great light; those who lived in a land of deep darkness—on them light has shined" (v. 2). These words carry a promise for anyone who has suffered through a sleepless night, for whatever reason, offering the hope that comes with the rising of the sun. The night is not forever, and morning will come. For Christians, this morning light is represented through the coming of Jesus Christ, the long-awaited Messiah.

A large hotel chain used a popular marketing slogan for years: "We'll leave the light on for you." It was their way of saying that they were going to welcome guests and be prepared to offer hospitality. I love the idea of a lighted beacon shining in the night—similar to what Isaiah's text describes today. Part of Isaiah's message reminds us, as people of faith, that no matter where we go, God will always leave the light on for us!

1. Today's symbol is a lamp. What does the symbol mean in the context of today's Scripture reading?

2. Consider a time when you metaphorically felt as if you were walking in the dark. What changed? How did you find hope to come through that time?

3. How have you experienced God's grace through another person metaphorically "leaving the light on for you"?

MONDAY

Creation
Genesis 1:1–2:3

During seminary, my Introduction to the Old Testament professor frequently offered up her own translation of the Hebrew text into English. When translating the creation story, she emphasized that standard English translations of God's response to creation were completely insufficient. She shared, with enthusiastic bravado, that God's response to creation could more accurately be translated by loudly exclaiming "Woah! This is soooo good!" Some of my classmates loved this translation so much that they named their intermural sports teams "Woah!" in acknowledgment of her enthusiastic teaching style.

In a world where so much seems to be broken, it is vital to both our psychology and our theology to remember that creation is inherently good. God was amazed with the goodness of creation as God was creating it. Every person you will ever meet (including yourself!) has been created in the image of God. As beings created in the image of the Divine, it is only appropriate that we also marvel in the goodness of the creation around us. All creation is a part of God's ongoing story.

We will wander into the fall of Adam and Eve tomorrow, but for today, we rejoice in the inherent goodness of God's created world, including us! God made all creation, and when God saw how good it was, God loudly proclaimed "Woah!" We don't have to look very far in the way the natural world works to share in this proclamation. While it's easy to see the bad aspects of humankind, remember that God also said "Woah! This is so good!" when God created us: you, me, and everyone you will ever meet.

Within this inherent goodness of creation, we find humankind in constant struggle with the Divine. The fall of Adam and Eve is really marked as the moment when humanity entered into a cycle of falling in and out of relationship with God and with one other, only to repent and seek restoration. But the promise of creation is the promise of right relationship—a covenant that Christians believe is reestablished through Jesus. Through Advent, we continue to anticipate the coming Christ, who represents the renewed goodness of God's original creation.

1. Today's symbol is a globe. Why do you think that is the symbol for the day? What does it mean?

2. What is the purpose of the creation story? How does it inform who we are, how we are called to care for creation, and how we are called to care for other human beings?

3. Pay attention to the world around you today and consider the entirety of creation. Name some things that make you say "Woah!" about God's incredible work.

TUESDAY

The Fall of Adam and Eve
Genesis 3:1–19

Yesterday we read about our Creator of the universe loudly proclaiming the goodness of creation: "Woah!!! This is so good!" When we get to chapter 3, the wheels fall off. Parts of the New Testament paint Eve as the one who bears the most guilt for the sins of humankind. Eve may have been the first, but she was far from the last. I find irony in Christian tradition casting Eve as the great villain when the characters in the story are playing the blame game with each other—one of the morals of this story is taking responsibility for our own mistakes and actions. Eve blames the serpent,

Adam blames Eve, and no one steps up and says, "Yep. It was me. I messed up—and I'm sorry."

In addition to accountability, this story is vital in that it is an origin story, teaching us about: (1) original or "inherited" sin, (2) the origins of death, and (3) the origins of shame.

The story of Adam and Eve introduces us to the idea of sin. Although the sin in this story is the disobedience of eating a fruit God had told the humans not to eat, we begin to understand what is meant by sin in the context of the Judeo-Christian God. While there have been a multitude of explanations of sin over the past three thousand years, my go-to definition simplifies sin down to anything that separates a person from God.

The second origin story contained in the narrative centers around the origins of death. Although there are trees still alive today that began growing before the pyramids were built in Giza, we know that nothing lives forever. All life has systems and cycles, and death is inherently a part of life. Since the scientific origins of death were shrouded in mystery for most of humankind's existence, the story of Adam and Eve offers up the origins of death impeding on God's perfect creation.

Even in this story, where God is incredibly ticked off because the humans ate a piece of fruit, God is still merciful. We are introduced to an inherent characteristic of God through God's benevolent mercy in this passage. God had assured the humans that they would die the moment they ate from the tree, and although they are now doomed to die after a life of toil, they are still allowed to live for a long time outside of the garden.

The third origin story contained in the narrative is the origins of shame. While the sensation of shame may be instinctive, defining what an individual considers shameful is a learned part of human society. Wanting to fit in and be accepted has vast evolutionary implications within our species—the benefits of fitting in to the group must have been evolutionarily advantageous to our ancestors. However, what makes a person fit in is purely a result of cultural context and learned behavior from one culture to the next.

I find it fascinating that those who composed this creation story did not consider shame to be part of God's good plan for creation. When Adam and Eve realize they are naked, they cover themselves in fig leaves—a very intentional narrative device on the part of the storyteller. There are a multitude of plants with which a human being could cover their nakedness, but the story chooses fig leaves—leaves known to be prickly—which would be most uncomfortable, especially on body parts with sensitive skin. The introduction of shame into the world came with its own disadvantages and discomforts, and the choice of fig leaf represents the discomfort that accompanies the sensation of shame.

What we find through this story is that the origins of sin, death, and shame are all tangled together in one narrative—much as they are throughout the story of humankind. Indeed, in Deuteronomy 30:19, we read: "I call heaven and earth to witness against you today that I have set before you life and death, blessings and curses." When we move toward God, we move toward faithfulness and fullness of life. When we move away from God, we move toward sin and death.

It can feel like the story of Adam and Eve is the moment when the wheels fell off for humankind, like the moment when everyone shrugs their shoulders and says, "It's all downhill from here." But we are part of the ongoing story in which humankind chooses between life and death, blessings and curses. We are a part of the ongoing story of choosing sin, but we are also part of the ongoing story of redemption and the mercy of God.

1. Today's symbol is a fruit tree. Why do you think that is the symbol for the day? What does it mean?

2. What is sin? What does it mean to commit an individual sin? What does the story of sin entering into the world tell us about God's mercy toward humankind?

3. For private reflection: What is a sin you struggle with? What about that sin draws you away from God?

How might you repent—a word that means "turn around"—and move back toward God?

WEDNESDAY

Covenant with Abraham and Sarah
Genesis 12:1–7; 17:1–8, 15–16

Anthropologists have established that in most regions of the ancient world, the average person never traveled more than ten miles from the location of their birth. With this knowledge, we can understand that the command from God to "go from your country and your kindred and your father's house to the land that I will show you" is akin to moving to another planet (12:1). Abraham and Sarah knew that when they had traveled that far from home, from the place of their origin, they would not see their loved ones again—or perhaps have any communication with them again. As a result, moving so far from home carried a death-like finality. When God asks Abraham and Sarah to move, this is not just a request for a change of address. God's request means that they will leave behind everything and everyone they have ever known, wandering into a great unknown world, with only God's promise as company.

The question is, even for the supremely faithful, why would these two people take this risk? To leave home and move to a new part of the world without the support of a community can still be terrifying in our time, despite being connected by cell phones and highways and airplanes. For them to venture out into the ancient world without a support system was not only frightening but also extremely dangerous.

However, we must keep in mind what God promises them for keeping their side of this covenant. In ancient Judaism, there was no belief in an afterlife. Throughout the Hebrew Scriptures, the souls of the dead descend into *sheol*, which was not a place of reward or torture, but a place of simple darkness and rest. In a faith without a strong sense of eternal reward or eternal life, the importance of leaving behind the legacy of many children becomes that much more important. Essentially, a person can achieve eternal life by having parts of themselves live on in their multitude of descendants. As Abraham and Sarah had not yet had even a single heir, there was great allure in God's promise that their descendants would become as "numerous as the stars of heaven and as the sand that is on the seashore" (22:17). Although we do not read from Genesis 22 for today's lesson, it is from that text that we get our symbol for the day: a sky filled with stars. Just as there are more stars in the sky than it is possible to count, Abraham and Sarah's descendants would be too numerous to count when God upholds the covenant.

There is a critical point that can be easy to miss in our text for today. Each time in Genesis that God reminds Abraham and Sarah of this covenant, God assures them that through their descendants, "all the families of the earth shall be blessed" (12:3). In other words, while Abraham and Sarah are blessed by this covenant, they are blessed that they might be a blessing to all the nations of the earth (22:18). The blessing is not to be confined to themselves and their descendants but to reach out across the world. Eventually, Christians believe that through our adoption into Abraham and Sarah's family through Jesus Christ, this blessing would extend to all the world as well.

1. Today's symbol is a night sky filled with stars. What does the symbol mean in the context of today's Scripture reading?

2. If you have ever moved away, what was it like leaving home? What was difficult about leaving? If you still live in your hometown, describe a time when you were homesick while traveling. What did you miss most about home? How did you respond when you got small tastes of home?

3. Name a time when you have taken a risk for your faith. How did it feel? What was at stake? Would you do it again?

THURSDAY

Moses
Exodus 3:1–15; 4:10–16

As the first of the Hebrew prophets, Moses' call story helped set the standard for the call stories of Israel's future prophets. Scholar Victor Matthews outlines a specific literary pattern for the calls of the prophets: (1) divine encounter or theophany, (2) an introductory word or greeting, (3) an objection or demurral, (4) a commissioning statement, and (5) a sign or talisman empowering the person who has been chosen.[3]

Moses encountered God through a burning bush. Theologians refer to this as a theophany, meaning a visible manifestation of the Divine to a human being. Through this encounter, God told Moses that the call is coming from the God of his ancestors. Moses objected to God's call, and God found ways to reject Moses' refusal. This was followed by a statement of what God called Moses to do, and then Moses received his staff as a sign that he would go forth and follow God's commission.

When Moses asks God's name, God responds "I AM WHO I AM" (Exod. 3:14). While this is an adequate translation of the Hebrew, because words do not always translate perfectly from one language to the next, it could also be translated "I will be who I will be." God's response is: "I am who I am" *and* "I will be who I will be." God cannot be put in a box and does not live into human expectations. God is the creator of the cosmos and cannot be confined.

It is easy for us to think of the characters in Scripture as more faithful than we are. We read the stories, think them over, and sometimes we gloss over the difficult parts that are contained within the text. In my experience, far too many people who believe Exodus is a sacred text fail to remember the full story of God's call on Moses' life.

Although a refusal or demurral is common in the call story of most prophets, it is typically used as a sign of humility, even though the prophet is willing to answer God's call. Unlike many other prophets who refuse God's call once in a show of humility, the repetition of Moses' refusal makes it seem quite genuine. When God asks, "Whom shall I send?" Moses is not standing at the front of the line waving his hand to enthusiastically volunteer as tribute. In fact, when we read the text closely, it looks more like he is cowering at the back of the line, trying to hide himself from being seen.

In the end, God must call Moses five times before Moses finally accepts the call. In Exodus 3:11, Moses asks "Who am I that I should go?" In verse 13, Moses implies that he cannot go because he does not know God's name. In Exodus 4:1, Moses insists that the people will not believe or listen to him. In verse 10, Moses insists that he is not a good speaker. And finally, in verse 13, he basically just begs God: "Please God, send someone else! Send anyone else!" Moses tries to get out of answering the call five times! This should give us all pause the next time we feel we are not fully living up to God's call on our lives.

Within Christianity, we often speak of clergy receiving God's call on their lives to full-time ministry. However, we do not speak as often of our common belief that once someone is baptized within the Christian faith, God places a call on that person's life. Although sometimes we think of a call from God as something unique or special, all baptized Christians have been called by the Divine. Sometimes we fall away from our divine purpose, but God consistently calls us back. As we continue our Advent journey, we look toward the Christmas story in which God uses ordinary people to change the world through Jesus. May we all have the courage to answer God's call as we continue onward toward Bethlehem.

1. Today's symbol is a burning bush. What does the symbol mean in the context of today's Scripture reading?

2. In what ways has God called you? How have you responded? Have you ever tried to say no to God? How might you respond in the future?

3. What does it mean to you that God's name in today's Scripture is *both* "I am who I am" and "I will be who I will be"? How might this transform our understanding of the Divine?

FRIDAY

The Passover/Escape from Egypt
Exodus 12:1–13, 29–36

After Moses was called by God through the burning bush, Moses traveled back into Egypt to fulfill God's command to lead the Hebrew people out of slavery and into the promised land. However, it took a long time to convince Pharaoh to set them free. Time and time again, Moses appeared before Pharaoh with the iconic line, "Let my people go." Each time that Moses was turned away with Pharaoh's refusal, God sent another plague on the land of Egypt. They faced nine different plagues: water turning to blood, frogs, lice, flies, livestock pestilence, boils, hail, locusts, and darkness covering the land. After the ninth plague, Moses warned Pharaoh that the final plague would be the worst of all.

Today's text addresses this tenth plague, in which the firstborn of every species in every household was killed. The Hebrew people were instructed to mark their doorposts with the blood of a lamb so that they would be passed over by the angel of death when the tenth plague struck the land of Egypt. Pharaoh, in his own grief over losing his firstborn son, finally relented and set the Hebrew people free.

Passover became the festival in which Jewish people annually celebrate their emancipation from Egypt. It is important to distinguish that through Passover, our modern Jewish siblings are not celebrating the deaths of those who were innocents in Egypt. In fact, at the annual Passover dinner, there is a moment of grief and naming of those who needlessly suffered through all the plagues, especially the final one. Instead, they are celebrating freedom and the downfall of a dangerous tyrant and dictator.

Today's Scripture serves two purposes in its context. First, it tells the story of the Hebrew people's flight from slavery in Egypt. However, the way this story is composed can also serve as an educational tool for teaching the story about the traditions that are kept as a part of Jewish observance of Passover. Part of the tradition includes a Seder meal, which is why today's symbol is a Seder plate. In the ritual meal, everything on the table tells the story of the Jewish people and their escape from Egypt. The traditional Passover table will hold *zeroa*, a roasted lamb-shank bone representing the lambs that were sacrificed as a part of the first Passover; *matzos*, unleavened bread, a symbol of how the Hebrew people fled from Egypt so quickly that they did not have time to allow their bread to rise; *charoset*, a mixture of apples, nuts, and spices symbolizing the mortar used by the Hebrew slaves as they toiled under the Egyptian taskmasters; *beitzah,* a boiled egg, symbolic of the festival sacrifice and of spring, when Passover takes place; *karpas*, parsley dipped into salt water, representing the tears of the enslaved Hebrews; and finally, *maror*, bitter herbs (most commonly horseradish in modern times) to remind the people of the bitterness of slavery.

The tradition of celebrating the Passover story has been sacred to the Jewish people throughout the ages, from the time before Jesus into the modern era. The celebration of Passover can offer a reminder of the resilience and faith of their ancestors while also acting as a reset for whom God calls them to be. Within Christian tradition, we also have a sacred meal that is essential to the story of our relationship with God: Holy Communion. Through Communion, we acknowledge this ongoing human cycle of turning away and back toward God. Frequently we do not want to associate the innocent little baby in the manger with the sacrificial lamb that the adult Jesus will become. However, even in the midst of Advent and the celebration of Christmas, it is vital that we remember the restorative opportunity for grace that Jesus brings into the world.

1. Today's symbol is a Passover plate. What does the symbol mean in the context of today's Scripture reading?

2. Why do you believe the tradition of observing Passover is still so important to modern Jewish people? Why does this story carry so much symbolism and significance?

3. There are parallels between the observance of Passover and the observance of Holy Communion. What parallels do you find between these two traditions? How does God use ordinary foods to inform us of the Divine?

SATURDAY

Zechariah
Luke 1:5–25

I have been told, throughout my life, that the natural setting for my voice is remarkably loud. As a child, I was drawn to activities in which no one told me to quiet down—my participation in sports, theater, and choir all come quickly to mind. As an adult, God called me to be a pastor who preaches and teaches. I firmly believe these two things are related; not once, in twenty years of ministry, has anyone ever complained because my sermon was too loud. My asthma and frequent respiratory infections mean that I tend to lose my voice at least once per year. When I lose my voice, I lose my primary form of communication, but I also temporarily lose a fundamental element of my identity.

Scripture doesn't offer commentary on Zechariah's feelings after he lost his voice for the length of Elizabeth's pregnancy. Despite this lack of commentary, he must have been frustrated by losing how he communicated, but it is logical that as a priest, preacher, and teacher, Zechariah also experienced some level of identity crisis upon losing the primary tool of his profession.

This story is our first from the New Testament. Both Zechariah and Elizabeth come from the priestly lineage described in great detail in the Hebrew Scriptures, a role and identity central to the faith and culture of the people of Israel. Throughout the stories of Hebrew prophets, there is an ongoing theme of special circumstances around the birth of a child destined to become a prophet, so Gospel writer Luke is careful to mention this priestly heritage as he sets the stage for Mary's relative Elizabeth and her husband, Zechariah, to have a son who would be a prophet similar to Elijah. Luke knows his Jewish audience will be familiar with this tradition and highlights the special circumstances around John's birth.

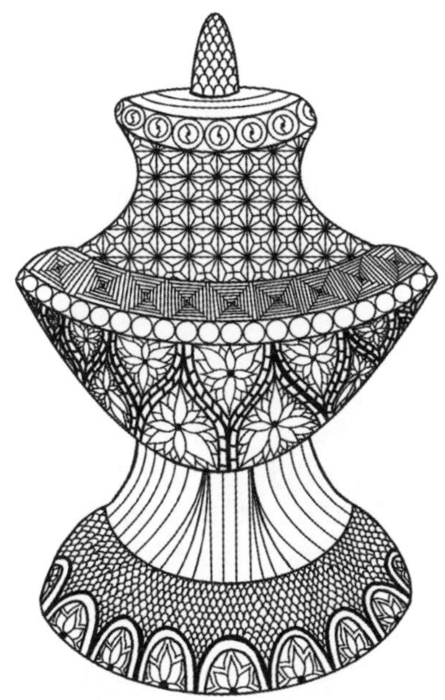

Although the roles are gender swapped, this story also calls to mind similarities with the proclamation that Sarah would give birth to Isaac. Sarah's response was to laugh in skeptical disbelief. In the same way, Zechariah did not believe the angel's proclamation that Elizabeth, who everyone believed to be barren, would conceive and give birth to a son.

Zechariah was chosen to offer incense at the altar, an incredible honor. The altar was located in front of the entrance to the innermost room of the temple, known as the holy of holies. At this time, the Jewish people believed that God's presence resided within the holy of holies, such that only the high priest could enter the holy of holies once a year. The high priest entered with his eyes closed, as they believed that witnessing the face of God would mean immediate death.

Zechariah went into the altar while the rest of the people and priests worshiped in the outer room. They believed that lighting incense was important to religious ceremony, as it created a cloud of fragrant smoke that was pleasing to God, and the smoke also offered a visible obstruction in the air, just in case the glory of God should appear. Many modern Christian traditions still incorporate incense into their worship services, and the burning incense is placed in a thurible, which is a metal container with holes that allow the smoke to be dispersed throughout the worship space.

Despite Zechariah's priestly position, he was still filled with doubt when he actually encountered a messenger of the Divine. The angel said that losing his voice for nine months was punishment for his disbelief. But it was also an ironic sign: the foretold son would be tasked with loudly preaching and proclaiming the coming of Jesus into the world. Luke makes it clear that Zechariah and Elizabeth had a lifelong pattern of faithfulness to Yahweh, but apparently even the angel's proclamation pushed Zechariah's faith to a point of disbelief.

Despite Zechariah's doubts, God did not withdraw this blessing the angel had promised. For those of us in the modern world, Zechariah's doubt can offer us hope in our faith journeys. All people of faith will experience mountaintop moments of faith but will also experience periods of time that feel like a "dark night of the soul," a phrase coined by St. John of the Cross. When we look to Scripture and find that even God's most faithful servants experienced this ebb and flow of faith, we can find hope for the highs and lows of our own journeys. As we continue to move toward Christmas, as we continue to come closer to the literal longest night of the year, we can remember that despite the patterns of our own spiritual ebbs and flows, God is constant and will never let us go.

1. Today's symbol is a thurible. What does the symbol mean in the context of today's Scripture reading?

2. Has there been a time in your own life when you have experienced a dark night of the soul or when you have

felt like Zechariah losing his voice? Do you find encouragement in knowing that even the most faithful people in God's greater story struggled with their faith? What hope does this bring you?

3. How have the stories of the ebb and flow of faith impacted your understanding of God's greater story of God's people and how God interacts with all creation?

Advent Week Three
Midwives of a Movement

Although Scripture spans many authors and eras, all these cultures were deeply rooted in systems of patriarchy. Across these cultures, women ranged in status from second-class citizens all the way to property considered less valuable than slaves. Regardless of their status, women were never perceived as equals to their male counterparts.

Throughout the books of the Bible, we see themes of patriarchy shine through in a variety of ways, but perhaps most prevalent is the comparatively few stories told about women or accounting for female perspectives throughout the text. There are many stories in which women who seem important to the story are never even named; Noah's wife is a prominent example.

Somewhat counterintuitively, there is also a constant thread throughout Scripture of God consistently siding with the oppressed. Time and time again, God stands against the oppressor, and on the side of those who have been oppressed, whatever their gender. This may be why the smattering of strong female characters we find in Scripture are those taking a stand against powerful men and unjust systems.

Jesus embodied God's care for the oppressed, including women, and he frequently empowered the women he encountered. The stories of Jesus' foremothers and other powerful women surely informed Jesus' treatment of women during his life. This week we will read several of those stories and see how God works through the underdog, the oppressed, those who are recipients of deep injustice at the hands of their fellow human beings. These are all stories of powerful women who changed the narrative, thereby changing the world. Through their stories we see how God weaves a greater story, one that will carry us all the way to the manger in Jerusalem, featuring the unlikely hero of the girl Mary. None of these women had physical strength or power, as the world understands it, on their sides—but they had the power of the Divine backing them up. How does the Divine work through unlikely heroes to continue the story, and how might we all see ourselves as unlikely heroes of God's greater story?

SUNDAY

Genealogy of Jesus
Matthew 1:1–17

> "Generations will reap what I sow.
> I can pass on a curse or a blessing,
> to those I will never know."
> –Sara Groves, "Generations"[4]

Hopefully, by this point in our Advent journey, some of the names you read in Matthew's genealogy of Jesus will be fresh in your mind. We have already read stories of Abraham, Isaac, Jacob, Judah, Jesse, David, and this week we will read the stories of Tamar, Rahab, Ruth, and Bathsheba. There are some names in the list that are familiar from other places in Scripture, like Hezekiah, Rehoboam, and Jehoshaphat. However, there are other names listed here that we find only by brief mention or in similar genealogical lists in Scripture. We do not know their stories or who they were.

Jewish tradition maintains that the dead are truly gone only once their names are no longer spoken, so the listing of ancestral names is vital to their continuing life. This is part of why we see so many of these lists within the Hebrew Scriptures. However, the list in today's Scripture serves a further purpose in establishing Jesus' identity. Jesus is firmly set as a descendant of a long line of prominent Jewish people. Matthew is setting the stage to prove that Jesus is the long-awaited Messiah that has been prophesized in Jewish theology. Through this genealogical list, Matthew is establishing Jesus as the heir to the covenant.

As we read through this list of Jewish men, it is fascinating that we find four women, three of whom are called by name: Tamar, Rahab, and Ruth. Rahab and Ruth are definitely not Jewish; they are included in the list as a part of the revelation that Jesus is more than just the fulfillment of Jewish prophecy but is a savior for the entire world, including the Gentiles. We are uncertain of Tamar's origins, although her heritage is presented in multiple ways in various Jewish lore. The fourth woman in the list is Bathsheba, though her name is not given; true to patriarchal norms, she is referred to in terms of her relationship to men. In this case, she is named as the mother of Solomon and (former) wife of Uriah. We will explore these women's stories this week, noting how remarkable it is that they are included in the lineage of Jesus.

1. Today's symbol is a family tree. What does the symbol mean in the context of today's Scripture reading?

2. Draw out the parts of your own family tree that you know off the top of your head. Who influenced you and helped make you who you are? How do you carry on the legacy of people in your family line? Traditions? Values? Faith? Physical traits?

3. Take some time to say aloud the names of the deceased who have influenced your life, including those beyond your traditional family. This can be a centering reminder of who you are and who you are called to be.

MONDAY

Tamar
Genesis 38:11–26

When we read about Sarah learning she would give birth to Isaac, we learned that in the culture of her time, bearing a son was considered an important part of a woman fulfilling her purpose. However, in a patriarchal culture in which commerce was managed by men and there was no social security net for senior citizens, having a son also meant that a woman knew she would be cared for in her old age, especially if she became a young widow. Daughters were sent away from their family units when they were married, but sons remained, and their wives joined the family compound. Having at least one son was essentially akin to how we save for retirement in our culture.

Judah, one of Jacob's sons with Leah—and half brother to Joseph—settled down, got married, and had several sons. Judah's oldest son, Er, married Tamar but died before she could bear a son. According to the law, when a married man died without children, his brother was obligated to marry the widow of the deceased, and their future children would carry the name of the deceased brother. Judah ordered his second son, Onan, to "perform the duty of a brother-in-law" (v. 8). Onan refused to do so and then also died. Judah blamed Tamar for the deaths of his sons. Rather than risking marrying her to his third son, Judah told Tamar that she could remain a widow until a time that Judah saw fit.

This left Tamar in a state of disgrace, without any sort of social safety net or financial security. However, we soon learn that Tamar is brilliant and cunning. She is not one to simply be mistreated and sent away quietly. She hatches a plan to get what the law has promised her, despite the bad-faith decisions of her father-in-law. Tamar disguises herself as a holy woman at a Canaanite temple, meaning that she is disguised as a temple prostitute. At Canaanite temples associated with fertility gods, it was common to have temple prostitutes on site to fulfill their practices of fertility rituals.

Judah went into a Canaanite temple—a problematic decision for someone claiming to follow Yahweh—and slept with Tamar in disguise. Because Judah was not carrying payment for her services, he agreed to leave her his signet and staff as collateral and then send her the payment of a lamb. When he tried to make the payment, she could not be found. When he soon discovered his unmarried daughter-in-law was pregnant, he became outraged, feeling that his family had been disgraced. Tamar then revealed that he was the father of her twin sons, and he realized that he had been outwitted, because Tamar could gain what she was legally owed only through an act of deceit.

King David descended from one of Tamar's twins, and so Tamar became a part of the story that leads to the birth of Jesus in Bethlehem. Tamar refused to accept oppression and injustice as the status quo and used the only asset she had available—her wits—to rewrite her own story. As we continue to journey toward the manger in Bethlehem, Tamar shows us how God works through the downtrodden and sides with the oppressed. The ministry of Jesus would eventually exemplify this same message through sermons like the Beatitudes, highlighting the ongoing theme of God's story: that the sacred kin-dom of God is not structured in any way like kingdoms of humankind.

1. Today's symbol is a lamb. What does the symbol mean in the context of today's Scripture reading?

2. How did Tamar seek out justice in a system that denied her justice?

3. Reflect on systems of oppression in our modern world. What are some ways you can actively combat those oppressive systems? How can God be at work within your life to establish God's kin-dom on earth as it is in heaven?

TUESDAY

Shiphrah, Puah, Jochebed, and Miriam
Exodus 1:8–2:25

Although the story of the infant Moses being sent down the Nile in a basket is an iconic part of biblical lore, many people may not be able to name the women in this part of the story, even though they are the main characters of the first chapter of Exodus. In a collection of books deeply based in patriarchal culture, when we see women named in Scripture, we know they are very important to the story.

The first women named in our text today are Shiphrah and Puah, the midwives who are serving the Jewish people enslaved in Egypt. Pharaoh had ordered the midwives to kill all newborn boys as soon as they are delivered and then report that the children were stillborn. Within the culture of Egypt at that time, the pharaoh was considered a god among the pantheon of other Egyptian gods. To disobey the pharaoh was not only disobedience of the law, it was also a matter of apostasy. Shiphrah and Puah are appalled at their orders from Pharaoh, but they knew that open disobedience to him could result in their own deaths. Rather than simply refuse his orders, they lied and told him they would do as he said—but instead, they did the opposite. When Pharaoh realized how many male infants were still being born, he called Shiphrah and Puah in to account. Their answer was a clever act of holy mischief at its best. I have often wondered if the person who wrote down the first two chapters of Exodus wrote with a smirk on their face, because the irony in this story is laid on thick, time and time again.

Egyptian culture, with an abundance of its own patriarchy, means that men were unlikely to be present for the birth of children—a man as important as Pharaoh certainly would not have been present for the birth of his descendants. Shiphrah and Puah insisted that the Jewish women were so hardy that by the time the two midwives received the call and arrived at the birthing site, all the babies had already been born and were in their mothers' arms. I can envision them shrugging their shoulders and asking, "What's a midwife to do?" Pharaoh had no basis on which to dispute their claim, so he ordered all infant males to be thrown into the Nile.

In the second half of today's story, the power of the pharaoh was once again thwarted through holy mischief by brave women. Moses' mother (later named in Exodus as Jochebed) delivered a healthy baby boy and was not willing to let the Egyptian soldiers take him away. She hid him for as long as she was able, and when she could no longer keep him hidden, she developed a plan to save him. She lined a basket with pitch to make it buoyant and watertight, set the child in the basket, and released it on the Nile (thus, in another ironic twist, actually following Pharaoh's mandate by putting her son in the river).

Moses' sister then followed him down the river. She is not named in those verses, but tradition usually has assumed that it was his sister Miriam, as she has such a large and prophetic role later in the book of Exodus. Miriam followed her brother, who was found by an Egyptian princess. In another stroke of irony, the princess decided to adopt the child, and Miriam piped up to ask if the princess needed assistance caring for the child. When she said yes, Miriam went and fetched their mother. Jochebed was then paid by Pharaoh's own palace to feed and raise her own son through infancy. The twists and turns, and God's sense of humor on display throughout this story, make it difficult to read without evoking a smirk on the face of the attentive reader.

The story of Jesus' infancy harkens back to this story, when another dictator, Herod, orders the death of Jewish infants in the region. The Holy Family escapes, ironically into Egypt, to save Jesus' life. Both Moses and Jesus were rescued from the hands of violent dictators and grow up to become redeemers for their people.

In the midst of the oppression of the Hebrew people, God uses the most unlikely characters to set the stage for their redemption. These brave women in Exodus became midwives of a movement that would set their people free, not through battle or physical strength but through intelligence, guile, and a spirit of holy mischief.

1. Today's symbol is a basket. What does the symbol mean in the context of today's Scripture reading?

2. Consider a moment in which the Spirit worked holy mischief in your own life. What were the circumstances? How was God working in unexpected ways?

3. This week's theme is midwives of a movement. How did today's Scripture help influence that title? What does it mean to midwife a movement?

WEDNESDAY

Rahab
Joshua 2:1–21

A generation after the powerful women we encountered in Exodus, we meet another brave woman: Rahab. After Moses led the people out of slavery in Egypt and they wandered in the wilderness for forty years, the Israelites finally returned to Canaan, the promised land. However, in the time since Jacob and his sons, the land had filled with other inhabitants. The first city they encountered was Jericho, and they hoped to conquer it. Joshua sent spies into the city for reconnaissance, where they encountered the Canaanite prostitute Rahab. Although Canaanite culture was also predominantly patriarchal, Rahab had established her own household within the city walls of Jericho. Rahab hid the spies on her roof among stalks of flax (the symbol for today), and in

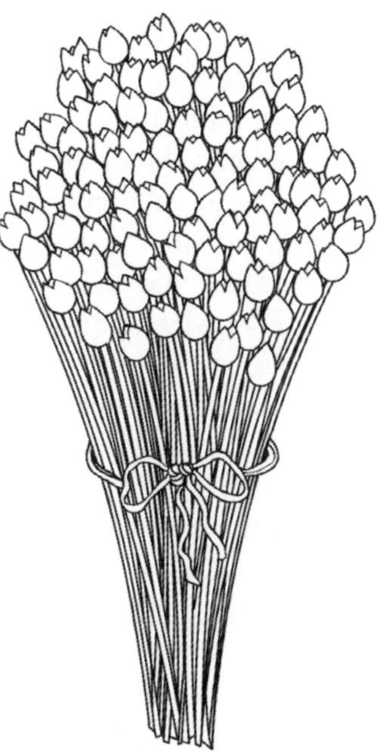

exchange, they agreed to spare her entire family when the city was destroyed.

Although Canaanites are repeatedly portrayed as bad and prostitution is repeatedly condemned throughout Scripture, Rahab becomes the hero of this story. The first act of a Canaanite toward the Hebrew people was one of hospitality. Rahab was a prostitute in the city of Jericho and was also powerful and intelligent, and she found ways to wield her own power in a society that sought to rob women of all power. How might we, in modern times, rethink the actions of oppressed persons as courageous acts of survival rather than judging them with our own narrow culture's standard condemnations?

The authors of the book of Joshua make it clear that God sided with Rahab—so much so that she became one of the women mentioned in the lineage of both King David and Jesus. Rahab found a way to be a protagonist among cultures that sought to relegate her to the role of unnamed extra. Despite her culture's best attempts to keep her in a background role, over two thousand years after her death, we are still discussing her name and her story. Rahab saw a path to agency and took advantage of it, claiming the narrative of her life as her own.

I grew up in the church singing in the children's choir, attending Sunday school every week, and participating in children's plays and programs. As a small child, I learned many songs with stories from the Hebrew Scriptures, such as "The Lord Said to Noah to Build an Arky, Arky," "Father Abraham Had Many Sons," and "Joshua Fought the Battle of Jericho." But no catchy lyrics or tunes taught me that there were powerful women in these stories as well. I understand why a story featuring a prostitute makes for difficult Sunday school fodder, but at the same time, we often clean up the Bible stories we tell children. A prime example: Noah becomes a cute story about animals on a boat rather than emphasizing the genocide of humankind and all the dead corpses floating in the water. Rahab's story could easily have been told without including her profession. And yet I did not encounter her story until I was a high school student deep in Bible study. The fact remains that, despite God and the writers of Scripture siding with Rahab, the modern church tends to judge her first by her profession rather than by her faithful acts toward God and God's people.

But perhaps Rahab's story is simply as dangerous in our time as it was in her own. God favored a woman who took control of her own story and claimed it for the good. And the cliché holds in Rahab's time as well as our own: well-behaved women rarely make history.

1. Today's symbols are stalks of flax. What does the symbol mean in the context of today's Scripture reading?

2. Today's text carries a lot of implications about women and their choices. Patriarchal culture inherently makes a lot of assumptions about women and their circumstances. How did Rahab use her circumstances for the greater glory of God? How could you use yours?

3. Spend some time contemplating who Rahab might have been. Explore her feelings and motivations in helping the Hebrew army overtake her city. Why did she make the choices she made? How was God a motivating force in her story?

THURSDAY

Ruth
Ruth 1:1–22

There is debate as to when the book of Ruth was written. The story is set in the time of the judges, but some scholars argue that this story was written and added to the Hebrew canon during the exilic period, when marrying and having children with non-Jews became a necessity for the survival of God's people. Some speculate that this story was added to the canon to encourage people to accept the children of these non-Jewish persons into the community.

Elimelech and Naomi were residents of Bethlehem until a famine struck, and they traveled to Moab to find food and care for themselves. While in Moab, Naomi gave birth to two sons: Mahlon, whose name meant "sickly," and Chilion, whose name meant "frail." The sons grew up to marry Moabite women, Ruth and Orpah. After a time, Elimelech, Mahlon, and Chilion all died, leaving the three women in crisis. A woman went from the household of her father into the household of her husband, and if she became a widow later in life, she was included in the household of her sons. Naomi now had neither husband nor sons. Ruth and Orpah, like Tamar, should have married their husbands' remaining brothers, but there were none. This is what Naomi was referring to when she said she had no more sons. Basically, the security net that was supposed to protect all three of them completely failed.

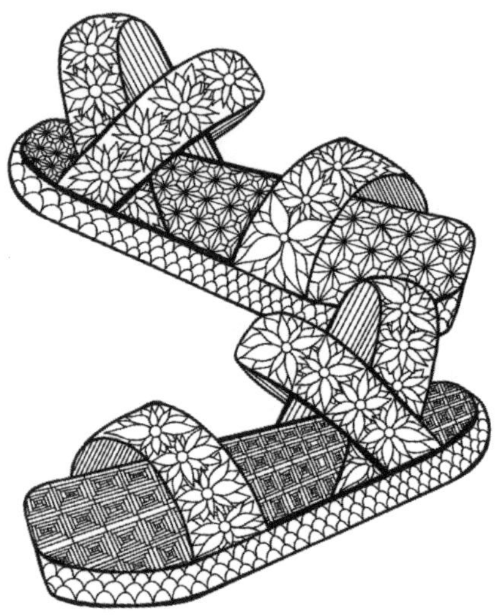

At this point, Naomi tried to send Ruth and Orpah back to their fathers' households, and she announced she would return to her own homeland. Orpah did so, but Ruth refused to leave Naomi's side. And she declared to her mother-in-law in the oft-quoted passage: "Where you go, I will go; where you lodge, I will lodge; your people shall be my people and your God my God" (v. 16).

Ruth walked with Naomi (who also names herself Mara, meaning "bitter") back to Naomi's original home in Bethlehem. Today's symbol is a pair of sandals, representing the shoes they most likely wore on their long journey together. They arrived at the time of the barley harvest, and as they were both widows, they went to the fields to glean what remained after the harvest. Laws in both Deuteronomy and Leviticus make it clear that when the time comes for harvest, faithful Jewish landowners are to leave some of their crop behind (either the second harvest, the gleanings, or the edges of the field, depending on the passage) so that widows and the poor can harvest it to feed themselves. Although not sufficient for survival, this was meant to help provide a small bit of safety net for those who were impoverished in ancient Israel.

This is how Ruth met Boaz, the landowner in the field she gleaned, who was related to her late father-in-law, Elimelech. Boaz was the son of Rahab and was open-minded about the goodness of people deemed outsiders. Boaz eventually took on the family obligation and married Ruth. This is how Ruth, a foreigner and outsider, became an ancestor of King David and, eventually, an ancestor of Jesus.

1. Today's symbol is a pair of sandals. What does the symbol mean in the context of today's Scripture reading?

2. What does it mean for Christians that a foreigner and outsider became one of Jesus' ancestors? What does this teach us about how God views all God's children, especially those who are labeled "foreigners" in our modern world?

3. Sometimes family is related by DNA, but sometimes we choose who we consider family. What does this story teach us about chosen family? What does it tell us about how chosen family can play a role in our spiritual lives?

FRIDAY

Bathsheba*

2 Samuel 11:2–17

***Author's note of caution**: Today's devotional contains open reflections on rape. If this topic is traumatic or sensitive for you, either read with caution or consider just spending some time in prayer and contemplation for today.

After Samuel anointed David, he spent years on the run from an angry and frightened King Saul. After Saul died, David finally took the throne. At first, it appeared he was going to be everything that King Saul was not: a good and righteous king. However, the phrase "power corrupts, and absolute power corrupts absolutely" is clichéd for a reason: it is, given the human condition, how humans behave. David fell into corruption like the first snowflake that begins a mighty avalanche—one small mistake led to enormous mistakes in time.

It is easy for us to miss David's first disgrace from our cultural perspective. During war in our time, most leaders remain safe from a distance or secure in a bunker; it is common for the leader in charge to coordinate their troops from a secure location. In the ancient world, the king's duty was to lead armies into battle, not to stay at home and coordinate from behind the scenes. David was, in the cultural norms of his own time, considered a cowardly and bad king for remaining in his palace while his troops marched off to battle.

Despite David failing to join them on the battlefield, Eliam and Uriah were clearly both known to David. Therefore, it was highly unlikely that he didn't at least know of Bathsheba. Instead of stopping when he learned that the woman bathing on the roof was Bathsheba, wife of one of his finest soldiers, he went ahead with calling her to the palace. In Hebrew, the word translated as "he saw" in verse 2 contains connotations of a predator stalking its prey and is most commonly used in this context rather than that of simply seeing.

When Bathsheba was summoned to the palace, she most likely assumed she had been called to receive notification of her husband's death in the war. She had no reason to believe she had been summoned for sex. In a strictly patriarchal monarchy, one does not simply say no to the king, especially when one's husband is under the king's command on the battlefield. Even if she did not protest, Bathsheba did not possess the autonomy to deny David's demand for sex.

This was not a consensual relationship as we've been given to believe. Even in my favorite study Bible, the heading of this text reads, "David Commits Adultery with Bathsheba," but this is a direct misrepresentation of the text. When one person is unable to say no to sexual advances, we call it rape. The passage should be labeled: "The Rape of Bathsheba and the Murder of Her Husband."

After this encounter, when Bathsheba sent word to David that he had impregnated her, David continued to dig down into the hole of corruption. He called Uriah back from the battlefield and ordered him to go home to his wife, assuming that they would sleep together and Uriah would be none the wiser when he came home to a new baby after the war. But Uriah, a man of honor, refused to go to the comforts of his home while his fellow soldiers were still fighting and suffering. And so David sent Uriah back to the battlefield carrying a message to Uriah's commanding officer: make sure that Uriah is killed in battle. Uriah went back to the battlefield carrying his own death sentence. Now that Bathsheba was a widow, David could claim her as one of his wives, and her pregnancy would bring no condemnation or shame.

Despite Bathsheba becoming an unwilling princess and the horrific nature of how she received that title, God works through this terrible situation to create something good. Bathsheba becomes one of the ancestors of the Messiah through David's line. This does not mean that everything happens for a reason—we will not justify rape by the child that is born of it. Rape is not a part of God's design in this world. However, God can use even the worst parts of life for fertilizer in the garden of God's kin-dom.

God designed a world in which even manure, with time and care, can be turned into the most fertile soil. So, too, it goes with our own lives and faith.

1. Today's symbol is a queen's crown. What does the symbol mean in the context of today's Scripture reading?

2. How do these stories speak to how God can turn life's manure into good soil?

3. What inspires you about the strength of Bathsheba? How can her story inform how you face adversity in your own life?

SATURDAY

Annunciation to Mary
Luke 1:26–38

Even though human beings are created in the image of God, God seems to enjoy reminding us that God does not view the world through our human lens. God's criteria for who might be best suited for a particular job looks vastly different than standard human criteria. We see this on full display when God chooses Mary to be the mother of Jesus, God incarnate.

If human beings were to plan God's incarnate arrival into the world, I suspect that the nativity scene would look far different than the one the Gospels portray. Mary was a young unwed woman as well as a Jewish person under the oppression of Roman occupation. She had little to no power in the world in which she lived. Viewed through the human lens, Mary seems like a poor choice to give birth to God Almighty incarnate.

Further, although Mary is engaged, she is not yet married. Her pregnancy would have been a scandal in her historical context. In her culture, when a couple was engaged, they did not live together and were not supposed to have sexual contact. However, engagement was still a legal arrangement, which meant all the steps of divorce were required in order to cancel a pending wedding.

This made Mary an even more unlikely choice, as her pregnancy had the potential to cause shame for both the families of Mary and Joseph as well as scandal throughout their small community. Yet, despite all the reasons to choose someone else, God decided Mary was the one who would bring Jesus into the world. Mary was chosen by God to carry this great miracle.

Throughout history, this scene has often been depicted with lilies in the background, because lilies are associated with purity and innocence. Because of these frequent depictions, the image of a lily has become closely associated with the annunciation to Mary in Christian tradition.

Gabriel stated that Mary is to name the child Jesus, a variation of the name Joshua, which translates to "one who saves." God's salvation turns out to be a far cry from the ideas of those who believed God was sending a great warrior to save Israel, but God has a way of working outside of human expectations.

Although Mary was afraid, she understood that God was asking her to be a part of the larger story of her people. Although it is a beautiful song, I often find myself annoyed when I hear the lyrics to "Mary, Did You Know?" which asks questions of Mary such as: "Did you know that your baby boy would one day rule the nations?"[5] My annoyance with the song is simply because the answer to each question posed by the song is a resounding yes! Mary knew exactly who Jesus was going to be; that's why she agreed to this event that turned her own life upside down. That was the whole point of the annunciation and the Magnificat! Mary understood that she was being asked to do a difficult thing, but she still responded with her own resounding yes!

As we continue our journey toward Bethlehem, spend some time today considering how God calls you. When, in your life, does it feel difficult to offer up a resounding yes to the Divine? Consider how you might move closer to God during this sacred season and how you might listen for God's voice in your life. Spend time contemplating how you might follow the example of Mary's story and bravely say yes when God calls your name.

1. Today's symbol is a lily. What does the symbol mean in the context of today's Scripture reading?

2. Reflect on a time when nothing went according to your expectations but things turned out OK in the end. How might this experience inform your life when it feels as if nothing is going according to your plans?

3. God frequently works through unexpected people in Scripture. Name a time when someone unexpected played an important role in your life or taught you something important.

Advent Week Four
Expecting Jesus

The Broadway musical *Wicked*, now a two-part film, is a retelling of *The Wizard of Oz* from the perspective of the Wicked Witch of the West. One of the frequent taglines used for the Broadway show has been: "So much happened before Dorothy dropped in."

Some Christians believe that the Hebrew Scriptures—also called the Old Testament—are separate from the story of Jesus. Not only is this belief false, but it was also declared heresy in the second century. Because of this dangerous trend within some Christian circles, I would like to repurpose *Wicked*'s tagline for the New Testament: "so much happened before Jesus dropped in." Alas, no one has put me in charge of promotions for the Holy Scriptures.

Jesus wasn't born into a vacuum but into the heart of the long story we've been exploring. Through the birth, life, teachings, death, and resurrection of Jesus Christ, God established a new covenant by which all the nations of the earth would be blessed—a fulfillment of God's original covenant with Abraham and Sarah.

As we enter the stories about Jesus this week, we continue to remember the stories that came before, and we also keep in mind that these same stories were still shaping Jesus' own culture and religious life. Because so much happened before baby Jesus dropped in.

The number of days in Advent varies from one year to the next, since Advent begins on a Sunday (which could be anywhere from November 27 to December 3) but always ends on December 24. As such, Christmas Eve will fall sometime during this week. As the number of days in Advent varies from one year to the next, this book has included enough devotions for a longer Advent. As such, depending on what year you read this book, there may be extra days provided.

SUNDAY

Magnificat
Luke 1:46–56

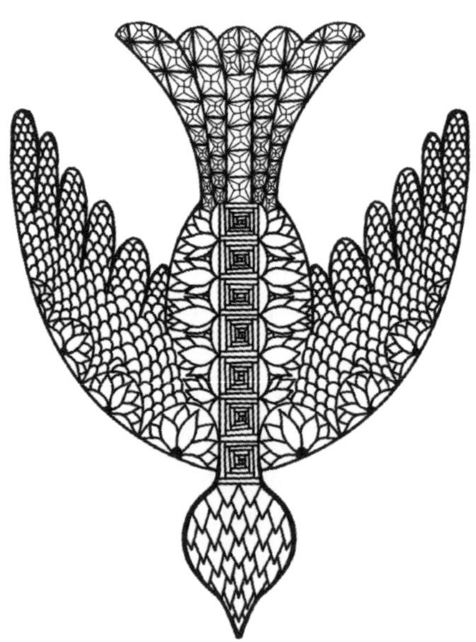

This passage is often referred to as the Magnificat, the Latin translation of Mary's first words here: "my soul magnifies." Sometimes this passage of prophecy is also referred to as "Mary's Song." Frequently used as a symbol of the Holy Spirit and a symbol of peace, our symbol for today is the dove, reminding us that Mary's prophecy in this passage predicts a day of peace for God's people.

And despite Mary's powerful and beautiful words of prophecy in this passage, it is easy to forget that in her context, her words wandered into the dangerous realm of treason.

Mary was a Jewish girl in a nation under foreign military occupation by the Roman Empire; she was an unwed teenager in a patriarchal culture controlled by a foreign patriarchal nation. Her brave proclamation dangerously turns the entire world order on its head. The idea that the powerful will be overthrown and the lowly will inherit the earth would have been terrifying words for those in power in Mary's time.

This week we will celebrate Christmas Day. While I deeply cherish the traditions that surround my annual celebrations of this holiday, I simultaneously recognize that modern American capitalism has deeply corrupted the celebration of God's inbreak into the world. It is uncomfortable to acknowledge, but if we take Mary's proclamation seriously, Mary's words are just as dangerous in our time; the majority of people who are measured powerful by human standards are rarely receptive to the naked truth. The idea of losing power or status terrifies those who possess it. All too often, this is a frightening message buried by Christianity in its American iteration; like the ancient Romans, we do not want to hear that the meek shall inherit the earth.

God chooses the unlikely to lead and to be in positions to fulfill God's work in this world. Although human beings are created in God's image, God's view of the world is quite different from that of humanity. Because of this, those who seek to follow Jesus are called on, time and time again, to assess our own worldviews. Are we viewing injustice and oppression in our world through the lens of the Divine, or are we viewing them through the lenses offered to us by the very people who perpetuate that injustice and oppression?

There are several sets of papers we have to write when going through the ordination process in my denomination. When I wrote my commissioning papers and went to my interviews, one committee member was very concerned about a theologian I had chosen to quote. He said that he was surprised I would use such a "cutting edge writer, who is frankly quite scandalous," instead of choosing to quote someone more "classic." I was shocked when I finally realized he was speaking of a quotation from Julian of Norwich, an English anchoress who lived and wrote during the fourteenth century. Julian speaks a lot about the motherhood of God, and the person on my interview team automatically assumed she must be a part of some modern radical feminist movement.

I began to reflect on the nature of the word *scandalous*, which multiple dictionaries essentially define as something which is shocking and/or offensive. I eventually decided that I wanted to live my life a scandalous woman of God—someone who was not afraid to speak the truth of the Divine, even if it causes upset or disturbance. Most nationwide and worldwide scandals are quickly forgotten; in fact, I can think of only a few in my lifetime that had staying power past a week or two. But, like Julian's work that can cause a scandal over four hundred years after her death, the gospel of Jesus Christ still ought to cause significant scandal to our modern world.

Embracing the message of Mary's Magnificat means reclaiming the scandalous message that all human beings are created in God's divine image and therefore have inherent worth; it means rejecting a cultural tenet of capitalism that argues that people can simply pull themselves up by their boot straps. How might you, like Mary before you, choose to the see the world through the eyes of the Divine and decide to live a scandalous life for God?

1. Today's symbol is a dove. What does the symbol mean in the context of today's Scripture reading?

2. Why were Mary's words scandalous in her own time and context? How might Mary's words be considered scandalous within our own time and context?

3. What does this Scripture tell us about who God is? What does this tell us about who we are?

MONDAY

Elizabeth Filled with Joy
Luke 1:39--45

When the Jewish people returned to Israel after their exile in Babylon, they rebuilt Jerusalem and the temple. The Jewish people ruled over themselves for more than 150 years, until the entire region was conquered by Alexander the Great and Israel and the surrounding countries came under Hellenistic (Greek) rule. Approximately 160 years later, the Maccabean revolt resulted in Israel reclaiming its independence, an act remembered into modern times through the Jewish holiday of Hanukkah. However, this new period of self-rule lasted only about one hundred years before the Israelities were conquered by the Roman Empire in 63 BCE.

By the time John and Jesus came into the world at the beginning of the first century, the Jewish people had been under oppressive Roman rule for more than a generation. The vast majority of Jewish people could not become Roman citizens, and so they had limited rights and opportunities even within the place they called home.

In the story of John's conception and birth, we once more find infertility at the heart of the telling. Elizabeth and Zechariah have been unable to have children, and they "both were getting on in years" (v. 7). The Gospel writer of Luke proclaims that they were both faithful to God but heartbroken at their inability to have children.

Zechariah was a priest, and one day when he was on duty, he delivered an offering to God. While doing so, the angel Gabriel appeared to tell him that Elizabeth would give birth to a son, and they were to name him John. The angel declared that John would be filled with the Holy Spirit and turn people toward God. Shortly thereafter, Elizabeth conceived a son and declared in verse 25, "This is what the Lord has done for me in this time, when he looked favorably on me and took away the disgrace I have endured among my people."

Between Elizabeth's pregnancy and today's Scripture reading, Mary was visited by Gabriel, who announced that she would also bear a child. In today's passage, Mary traveled to visit Elizabeth, a member of her family. When she saw Mary, "Elizabeth was filled with the Holy Spirit and exclaimed with a loud cry" (vv. 41–42) and then began to prophesy. This language closely mirrors language that references prophets in the Hebrew Scriptures. It is important to understand that both Elizabeth and Mary are proclaiming prophecy throughout Luke 1. Elizabeth saw with great clarity beyond the here and now. She was not the least bit concerned or judgmental about her young relative's pregnancy, despite the fact that Mary was unwed. From the perspective of their culture, Mary's pregnancy was a huge embarrassment to the entire family—something that could have brought shame on them all. But Elizabeth had seen a vision of the bigger picture, and she understood the great significance of the child Mary was carrying in her womb.

"When Elizabeth heard Mary's greeting, the child leaped in her womb" (v. 41). Even from his mother's womb, John was compelled to carry out his calling to proclaim that the time had come when God would save God's people. John was the messenger who prepared the way for the ministry of Jesus, and John fulfilled this role, even in utero.

Mary and Elizabeth were elated at the news the angel Gabriel brought to their family: the time had come when God would save God's people—they were anticipating the day when they would have full autonomy in the land in which they lived. Today's symbol is a king's crown, representing the lordship of Jesus Christ in Elizabeth's delighted words: "And why has this happened to me, that the mother of my Lord comes to me?" (v. 43). As women living in a patriarchal culture that was also under Roman occupation, they were oppressed on multiple levels. They had many reasons to celebrate that the day had finally come when they would be set free.

1. Today's symbol is a king's crown. What does the symbol mean in the context of today's Scripture reading?

2. Name some ways that oppression exists in our modern world. God consistently sides with the oppressed throughout Scripture. How might Christians be called to resist oppression in the world today?

3. How do you think Elizabeth's wisdom could have been an incredible blessing to her cousin Mary? How do we share our hard-fought wisdom with those who follow us?

TUESDAY

A Young Woman
Isaiah 7:10–17

Today's passage comes from Isaiah and describes an interaction between the prophet Isaiah and King Ahaz of the Southern Kingdom (Judah). (Matthew would eventually list King Ahaz in the genealogy of Jesus.) In today's Scripture reading, Judah was facing an imminent invasion by the armies of Israel and Syria, who joined together against Judah because Judah refused to aid them in their stand against the Assyrian Empire. Ahaz was contemplating making a deal with the Assyrian king and thereby selling out his neighbors, and the prophet Isaiah was trying to talk him out of this course of action.

Even though today's Scripture is often used in a Christian context of prophesying the coming of Christ, in its original context, Isaiah was using the birth of the young child as a sign. He was pointing to a young woman about to give birth and arguing with Ahaz that by the time the child was old enough to know right from wrong, both Israel and Syria would fall to the Assyrians—Ahaz did not need to sell out his neighbors but simply wait on their inevitable destruction. "He shall eat curds and honey by the time he knows how to refuse the evil and choose the good" (v. 15) is Isaiah saying that if Ahaz only waited and trusted in God, the child about to be born would live in plenty—a land flowing with milk and honey.

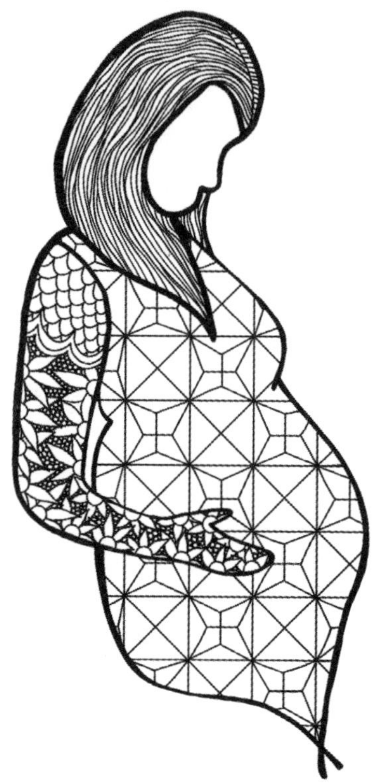

Eventually, Ahaz ignored the prophet's advice and made a deal with the Assyrians, paying homage to their king, and both Israel and Syria fell to the onslaught of the Assyrian armies. Ahaz became a vassal for the Assyrians, further weakening the kingdom of Judah, which eventually fell to Babylonian invaders. Thus, Ahaz is remembered as one of the evil kings of Judah, even offering his own son as a burnt offering to the Assyrian god Moloch.

At first glance, it seems that Ahaz refused a sign from God out of piety—after all, the faithful are not to put God to the test. However, both the prophet and further reading reveal that Ahaz refused to accept a sign from God not out of faithfulness but out of a desire to go through with the plans he has already made. He ignored God's sign because he did not want his mind to be changed.

Using Isaiah as a mouthpiece, God commanded Ahaz to trust in the Divine—even going so far as to proclaim that the woman about to give birth would bear a child named "God is with us" (v. 14). Ahaz was surrounded by reminders that God is present, that God was still at work within the kingdom of Judah, but Ahaz refused to see the Divine at work in front of his own eyes.

This inability to see the Divine at work was not, however, limited to ancient kings. An inability to see or hear the good news is an ongoing part of the human story, from the fall in the garden of Eden all the way into our present era. As we look to the coming of Christ, we remember that we are part of this greater, ongoing story of the Divine. As you read tomorrow's Scripture passage from the Gospel of Matthew, pay close attention as Matthew refers to these verses from Isaiah. Matthew's quotation from Isaiah has closely linked Isaiah's prophecy to the birth of Jesus within modern Christianity. While the story of how Isaiah's prophecy is fulfilled is contained within the book of Isaiah, it is possible that prophecy can have more than one fulfillment, as God's story with humankind has always been an ongoing work in progress. This Christmas, keep your eyes open for the ongoing work God is continuing to do in the world and for times when the Divine still speaks. Keep your ears and your heart open for the good news of Jesus Christ.

1. Today's symbol is an expecting mother. What does the symbol mean in the context of today's Scripture reading?

2. Have you ever refused to believe something because you didn't want to change your mind? What were the circumstances? How did you finally reconcile with the truth of the circumstances?

3. Our text today was a prophecy written in a particular time for a particular audience. That said, prophecy can also have more than one fulfillment. Spend some time reflecting on how these two things can be simultaneously true.

WEDNESDAY

Birth of Jesus
Matthew 1:18–25

While modern Christians understand marriage as a covenantal relationship (and some traditions recognize it as a sacrament), modern marriage is also a legal arrangement; this is why a lawyer—a legal expert—is almost always needed in matters of divorce. Before that marriage license is signed, however, there is no legal process for calling off an engagement.

At the turn of the first century, engagement was considered a legally binding relationship. However, engaged couples did not reside together until they were officially married, which also meant that couples were not supposed to engage in sexual contact until marriage ceremonies were complete. Although Mary and Joseph were not yet married, their engagement was a legally recognized union under Jewish law—meaning that Joseph would have to go through the process for a divorce if he decided to leave Mary. He couldn't just call off the wedding, as an engaged person could do in the twenty-first century.

The implication in the text is that because Joseph and Mary

have not lived together, they have not yet engaged in sexual activity. I say implication even though Mary is referred to as a virgin in most English translations, because the word is a marked decision by translators of the text. This passage directly quotes yesterday's passage from Isaiah, and the Hebrew word *almah* as it is used in Isaiah means "a young woman ready for marriage," so it could be translated as "young woman" or as "virgin." However, there are separate Greek words for these two ideas, as there are in English. The translators of the Septuagint, a translation of the Hebrew text into Koine Greek, made an editorial choice to translate the Hebrew *almah* as *parthenos,* "virgin," instead of *koré,* "young woman." The writers of the Gospels had access to the Septuagint, and this translation choice carried over to the New Testament.

Since Mary and Joseph have not yet engaged in sexual activity together and Mary is pregnant, the obvious conclusion for Joseph is that Mary cheated on him with another man. Joseph had two options: he could divorce her publicly or privately. A public divorce would have meant accusing her of adultery, and the punishment for both men and women who committed adultery under Jewish law was to be stoned to death. A private divorce would mean calling off the wedding but ensuring that her life would be spared. The text says he had already chosen to divorce her but had decided to do it privately, thereby sparing her life.

Like Joseph's namesake from Genesis, God spoke to Joseph through a dream. An angel appeared to Joseph in his dreams, assuring him that Jesus' conception was a divine event and that Joseph should still agree to become Mary's husband. They were to name him Jesus, the Greek form of Joshua, which means "the Lord saves" or "Yahweh helps."

Joseph and Mary are called on to continue God's ongoing story by joining together to raise Jesus into adulthood. Jesus comes into the world to establish a new covenant with God's people, as a crucial part of God's salvific work in the world. The stories of the Torah were clearly fresh in the minds of both Joseph and Mary as we read the story told in the Gospels of Matthew and Luke, and both answered God's call to join in the greater story of God's love.

1. Today's symbol is an angel. What does the symbol mean in the context of today's Scripture reading?

2. Before the dream with the angel, Joseph was still planning on showing Mary grace by means of a private divorce. How does this exemplify the character of the person God chose to become Jesus' earthly father?

3. Mary and Joseph had many preparations to make before Jesus was born. This Advent, you have spent a lot of time studying Scripture. How has that time prepared you for the joy of Christmas Eve and Day this year? How do you feel more prepared for the spiritual joys of Christmas?

THURSDAY

Jesus Born in Bethlehem
Luke 2:1–7

We are culturally attuned to the idea of there being no room at the inn when Mary and Joseph arrive in Jerusalem. Most English translations of Scripture have included a version of this phrase. However, Luke 2:7 in the NRSVue reads, "And she gave birth to her firstborn son and wrapped him in bands of cloth and laid him in a manger, because there was no place in the guest room." This is likely a more faithful translation of the Greek word *kataluma*, although this may disrupt some modern readers' carefully cultivated narratives, especially anyone who played the role of innkeeper or innkeeper's wife in a childhood nativity play.

Bethlehem was far too small to have had an inn, so the text likely refers to a household in town that was large enough to have a guest room used by the occasional traveler. We see *kataluma* used later in Luke 22:11, when the disciples are seeking a room in which to have their Passover meal the night before Jesus' death. There it has always been translated as a "guest room," making this an inconsistency in translation in which the traditions surrounding a mistranslation have often won out over accuracy.

In ancient Bethlehem, most homes consisted of a two-story edifice. The first floor was an area used for keeping livestock enclosed and safe during the night, much as we might use a barn in the modern era. In these two-story ancient homes, the family lived in the residential area on the second floor. Although the language "guest room" is used, the text clearly states that Jesus was placed in a manger. The proximity of the manger makes it possible that they were housed on the first floor of a home, alongside the livestock—or they might have been in a spare room that also doubled as a storage space.

Despite the disruptions to the narratives that have thrived in our culture, Mary and Joseph's lodgings were still clearly extremely humble in quality. When we envision how the creator of the cosmos might come into the world incarnate, human imagination would select a far more regal welcome into the world—one that includes palaces, grand entrances, and plenty of gold shining all around. A humble birth by an unwed teenage girl in a middle-of-nowhere town and then being placed in a livestock feeding trough with hay—this is certainly not the stately entrance into the world that any of us would plan for the Divine.

But Jesus did not come into the world to bring good news for the elite and wealthy; Jesus' message of good news was for all humankind—including ordinary, everyday folks. God was determined to live among human beings despite all the messiness that comes with our reality. But the story of Jesus does not end in the final word of Revelation—the story of Jesus continues in the hearts and lives of all who seek to follow him in the present. Through baptism, Christians join an ongoing and eternal story of the Divine.

1. Today's symbol is a manger. What does the symbol mean in the context of today's Scripture reading?

2. Consider a time when you desperately wanted to be near to someone you love. Why does presence matter to us? How did God understand the importance humans place on presence?

3. Have you ever looked around your workspace, home, or life and thought "This is a mess!" What does it mean to you that God chooses to be with us, even in the mess?

FRIDAY

Shepherds Visit Jesus
Luke 2:8–20

When I graduated from seminary, I served for a while as a chaplain in a large hospital. When I was the on-call chaplain, I could be called to any section of the seven hundred-plus bed facility. We were automatically a part of the team called to respond anytime there was a level I or II trauma arriving at the hospital or anytime there was a code blue (a patient's heart stopped). Because of this, our keys could open most locked sections of the hospital—multiple intensive care units, the emergency department, etc. It was not unusual to be called all over the hospital in a single twenty-four-hour shift. However, security was so tight in the maternity ward that chaplains had to be buzzed in when we were called for emergencies. I was frequently impressed by how tight the security was when entering the maternity ward.

Jesus, however, was not born in a sterilized hospital room. Jesus was born while Mary was on the road away from home, and Jesus was placed in a livestock feeding trough instead of a cradle. And then come the shepherds. The phrase "shepherds living in the fields" (v. 8) indicates that these were not wealthy flock owners but were instead the hired help caring for the livestock. As they were sleeping in the fields, it is entirely possible that these men, while employed, were homeless. Since they were sleeping in the fields among the sheep, it is also safe to assume that they were not walking around in a well-groomed state. If we translate this into American culture, God didn't send modern,

Midwestern, salt-of-the-earth farmers in to see the baby Jesus. God sent rough-and-tumble, just-got-in-from-weeks-on-the-range cowboys. The shepherds were most likely completely unwashed, dirty, smelly, and rough around the edges—complete with bad language to match. It is unlikely that the shepherds would have made it past security in a modern maternity ward. In Luke's Gospel, the first people invited to meet Jesus were not scholars or priests or royalty but rather dirty field workers who their upper-class contemporaries would have deemed as unfit company.

It is worth noting that Zechariah, Jesus' uncle, is the only religious official to whom a heavenly messenger appears in either Christmas story as told by Matthew or Luke. Messages from the Divine are not conveyed to a temple full of priests and religious scholars. Instead, God appears to the ordinary (Mary and Joseph), the lower class (shepherds), and even ritually unclean foreigners (the magi).

What does it mean that our God chooses such humble beginnings, when God could have chosen to come into the world anywhere, at any point in history? Part of what it means is that God understood the messiness of being human: the grit, the pain, the blood, the suffering—all that comes with being human. Despite all these things, God chose to be with us, and because that embodiment mattered so much, God did not shy away from the mess.

The story of redemption shifted significantly for all the people of the world through the inbreak of God's kin-dom in Bethlehem. The first covenant had been reserved for the children of Abraham and Sarah, but this new covenant would be open to all the persons of the world.

1. Today's symbol is a flock of sheep standing in a field. What does the symbol mean in the context of today's Scripture reading?

2. Who might God invite to the manger if Jesus were born in our modern world? Who might we overlook that God would still remember?

3. How might desanitizing your visualization of the nativity help desanitize your understanding of God with us? Have you ever had a particularly messy Christmas? How was God there, in the midst of the mess?

Twelve Days of Christmas and Epiphany

The Covenant: Promise of Past, Present, and Future

Throughout the twelve days of Christmas and Epiphany, we will explore the covenant God established through Jesus Christ—both the origins of that covenant as well as the ongoing covenant Christians are adopted into through baptism. God's greater story is an ongoing epic in which we are all called to be participants.

Most Christian denominations maintain the doctrine of the Trinity, the idea that God is three in one and one in three. Traditionally referred to as the Father, Son, and Holy Spirit, sometimes the Trinity is also referred to as Creator, Redeemer, and Sustainer. Regardless of the language chosen by your tradition, you are probably familiar with this idea.

Because of the tradition of the Trinity, the story of Jesus doesn't begin in Bethlehem, it begins in Genesis when God creates heaven and earth. The story of Jesus doesn't end with the ascension or even with the final word of Revelation. The story of Jesus continues in the stories of those of us in the modern world who try to follow the path of Christ.

CHRISTMAS DAY

The Word
John 1:1–18

Poetry is used to convey something beyond the words on the page—ideas or concepts that are too big to put into words. Poetry moves us with unexpected wordplay and clever juxtaposition of sound. It is wise to approach today's Scripture as the beautiful poetry that it is. However, poetry often works because language is imprecise and because a single word can have multiple meanings. Unfortunately, this creates significant difficulties for translators when trying to translate from one language to another.

We find an excellent example of this in Lin-Manuel Miranda's song "My Shot" from the musical *Hamilton*. The chorus of the song repeatedly sings, "I am not throwing away my shot." In English, the word *shot* has multiple meanings, several of which are implied during the performance of this song. When "my shot" is sung in the chorus, some American Sign Language translators will use a different word for shot each time. They use one sign that means taking a shot of an alcoholic beverage, one sign that means opportunity, and one sign that means shooting a gun. They do this because all these various meanings are implied in the original English musical performance, but there is no sign in ASL that represents all three of these meanings simultaneously.

In the same way, when John 1 is translated into English from Koine Greek, although the translators do their best, they cannot help but lose some of the meaning that would have existed for the original readers of the text. A lot is lost in translation. The author in John 1 used the word *logos* in multiple ways that would have been recognizable to readers within the culture of that time. The beginning of the book, which starts with "in the beginning," would have drawn all Jewish listeners to think of the first verse of Genesis, which begins in the same way. Thus, John drew listeners into the creation story from the get-go, as all creation exists through God's spoken word. John utilized *logos* as a means of invoking wisdom as it is conveyed throughout Jewish Scriptures. John's use of *logos* is also a play on Greek philosophy, which used the word to refer to a rational and divine intelligence, an omnipotent truth that exists throughout the universe. One theologian writes: "The Word in John evokes the creative word of Genesis 1, the cosmic and rational word of Greek philosophy, the word of Wisdom and Torah from Hellenistic Judaism, and the person and story of Jesus . . . Thus, Jesus is Wisdom, Torah, reason, and the ordering force of reality."[6]

John's use of *logos* indicated more than the simple incarnation of the Divine. The *logos* represents the inbreak of God's kin-dom into the physical world. We have spent the last four weeks preparing our hearts, souls, and minds for this miraculous inbreak. The day has arrived; the celebration has begun! But Christians are not mere bystanders attending the celebration but are called to be participants in the ongoing story of the Divine. The inbreak of God's kin-dom is an ongoing event. How will we commit to this *logos*, this ongoing telling of truth, this ongoing ordering of the universe toward the kin-dom of God? The good news of "God with us" is not one to be reserved for December 25 but a way of living our lives in the world that everyone we encounter might experience the love of God through the way we live our lives.

1. Today's symbol is the word *logos* in Greek letters. What does the symbol mean in the context of today's Scripture reading?

2. How does the opening of John's Gospel continue the arc of the story we read through the Hebrew Scriptures? How is Jesus a continuation of this same story?

3. Reflect on the most meaningful part of your Christmas celebration this year. What was it? How do you see God reflected in the practice?

DECEMBER 26

Birth of John the Baptist
Luke 1:57–80

In today's Scripture, we encounter Zechariah in Luke's Gospel for the first time since the announcement of Elizabeth's pregnancy. Zechariah was unable to speak throughout his wife's pregnancy because he doubted that God would do as the angel said. When John was eight days old, Elizabeth and Zechariah visited the temple, both to have the baby circumcised and to observe the postpartum cleansing rituals that Judaism required of Elizabeth. Luke knew it was important to mention the faithfulness of Elizabeth and Zechariah, and he demonstrates this with the actions they took to follow Jewish traditions.

Elizabeth told the temple officials that the child would be named John, as Zechariah had been told when he was visited by the angel. The officials were shocked, as this was not a traditional name in Zechariah's family. Zechariah indicated that he also wanted this to be the name of their son. It is at this moment that he was able to speak again for the first time since learning about the pregnancy.

Despite Zechariah coming from a priestly family line and the fact that he served as a priest at the temple, Zechariah spoke in this passage as a prophet rather than a priest. Luke has multiple examples of people being filled with the Holy Spirit and speaking words of prophecy in the first two chapters of the Gospel. We see Elizabeth, Mary, Simeon, Anna, and Zechariah all filled with words from God for God's people between the beginning of chapter 1 and the end of chapter 2.

In the verses following today's Scripture, Luke 2 records that all this took place during the time of Augustus ruling as the Roman emperor. Augustus was well known for promoting *pax romana*, or "Roman peace" during his reign, and Zechariah's words come at the end of chapter 1 as a literary device set intentionally to cast God's peace in juxtaposition to the forced peace purported by the empire. But it is clear that a true desire for peace was as radically countercultural in Rome as it is in our modern era. In 1:78–79, we read:

> Because of the tender mercy of our God,
> the dawn from on high will break upon us,
> to shine upon those who sit in darkness and in the shadow of death,
> to guide our feet into the way of peace.

The peace that Zechariah prophesies will break like the "dawn from on high," much like a sunrise breaking the horizon at the end of a long and cold night. While the depths of night offer a time for rest and peace, the breaking of a new day implies that the time has arrived to get up and begin life's work once more. The difficult work of those who seek to follow in the path of Jesus will be the hard work for peace, the building of God's now-but-not-yet kin-dom here on earth.

1. Today's symbol is the sunrise. What does the symbol mean in the context of today's Scripture reading?

2. Describe a beautiful sunrise you have witnessed. What was special about it? How did it make you feel? What were the circumstances that caused you to pause and notice the sunrise on that day?

3. What does it mean to do the hard work of peace in our world? What might we be called to sacrifice in exchange for that sort of peace?

DECEMBER 27

Preparing the Way
Mark 1:1–8

The beginning of Mark is an indication of what we will find throughout Mark's Gospel. Unlike Matthew or Luke, he is not concerned with the birth of Jesus or John. Unlike the Gospel of John, he does not begin with beautiful poetry that captures the mind and soul. Mark's approach is simple: get straight to the point while being as succinct as possible.

The wilderness (where we find John in this passage) is frequently referred to as a place of renewal in Scripture. This is ironic, given that wilderness in the ancient world would have been far more dangerous than most places we consider wilderness in our modern world. Being in the wilderness in the ancient world would not have been the same as us walking through a national park—there were wild animals, including far more abundant and dangerous predators, as well as any number of untold dangers from other human beings. The quote in this passage is from Isaiah 40:3—a word to the people in exile to build a road toward Jerusalem for their return home. In context, these words indicated that the time of restoration is drawing near.

John appeared in the wilderness, by the Jordan River, baptizing all the people who came to him. However, as the practice of baptism does not exist in Judaism, and clearly John was Jewish, how did he come to baptize people at all? Most major religions have some practice of ritual cleansing involving water. While the rituals may look quite different from one tradition to the next, this practice of using water in a ritualized manner is incredibly common across the world. Judaism is no exception, and there are several references to ritualistic cleansing found in the Hebrew Scriptures. However, the practice of baptism seems to be a new phenomenon in the centuries that pass from the final book of the Hebrew canon to the turn of the first century. Under the influence of Greek and Roman traditions, and most likely under the influence of Zoroastrianism, some Hellenistic Jews began the practice of baptism around the turn of the first century. Obviously, John the Baptist was one such Jewish person who began utilizing this practice. Baptism eventually became a Christian practice over time, and while our modern Jewish siblings still practice ritual purification with water, they no longer practice an act that should be referred to as baptism.

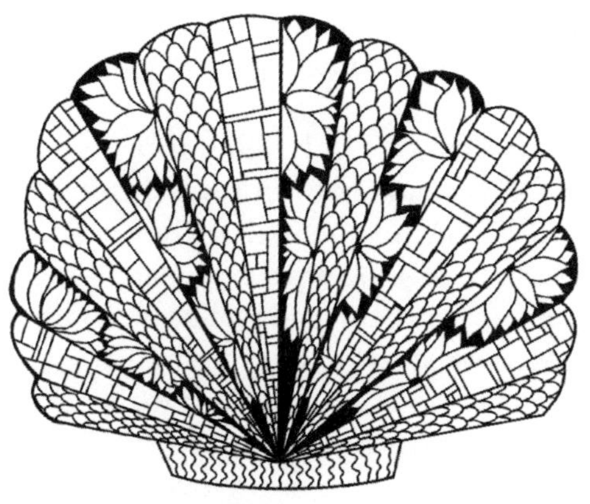

The masses were coming to hear John preach and to have him baptize them, but John repeatedly makes clear that he was but the messenger: "The one who is more powerful than I is coming after me; I am not worthy to stoop down and untie the strap of his sandals" (Mark 1:7). He quotes Isaiah 40:3–4:

> A voice cries out:
> "In the wilderness prepare the way of the Lord;
> make straight in the desert a highway for our God.
> Every valley shall be lifted up,
> and every mountain and hill be made low;
> the uneven ground shall become level,
> and the rough places a plain."

This passage in Isaiah was being written from the context of Babylonian exile and was a call to comfort the people in exile, assuring them that they would eventually return to Jerusalem—God would prepare a highway that was straight and flat for them to travel home. The first constructed roads archeologists have found date back to around 4000 BCE in ancient Mesopotamia. And while a road that is straight and flat might not seem that impressive to those of us living in Midwestern states in the twenty-first century, keep in mind that at this point in history, the vast majority of roads were still simple foot paths composed of earth that was well worn by humans and animals.

Today's symbol is a shell, which has long been a symbol associated with baptism. Some traditions and churches even practice baptism with the priest or pastor using a shell to scoop water over the head of the baptized rather than drawing water with the hand.

1. Today's symbol is a shell. What does the symbol mean in the context of today's Scripture reading?

2. What is your tradition's understanding of baptism? Do you remember your own baptism? What words were used? Read your tradition's baptism liturgy if you can.

How do you find God at work in this intersection between the physical and the spiritual worlds?

3. Why is Mark quoting this particular passage from Isaiah? Why did Mark find it relevant to the beginning of Jesus' ministry?

DECEMBER 28

Jesus Presented at the Temple

Luke 2:22–24

Today's Scripture reading may be very short, but its background makes up for its brevity. After the Babylonian exile, the temple in Jerusalem (sometimes known as the Second Temple) was rebuilt, and the temple rituals of the Jewish people began to resemble their practice prior to the exile. Unlike our era, where I might pass by multiple houses of worship to arrive at the one where I am going on Sunday morning, the Jewish people of that time firmly believed in the importance of visiting the temple in Jerusalem at least once a year and would travel there for sacred ceremonies.

When Jesus was eight days old, Joseph and Mary took him to the temple for circumcision and for Mary to observe the postpartum Jewish cleansing rituals.

The rituals mentioned in today's text actually come from three different locations in the Hebrew Scriptures. In Exodus 13:12–13, God orders Moses that among God's people, they "shall set apart to the LORD all that first opens the womb. All the firstborn offspring of your livestock that are males shall be the LORD's. . . . Every firstborn male among your children you shall redeem." Therefore, all firstborn males were to be presented at the temple and redeemed with a sacrifice.

It is clear, in context, that Jesus was brought to the temple to be circumcised. A multitude of theories abound about how circumcision became a marker of God's covenant with Israel, but it is enough to know that Genesis 17:12 requires "throughout your generations every male among you shall be circumcised when he is eight days old." Thus, the covenant was maintained with an outward and visible sign of an inner commitment to the God of Abraham and Sarah.

As a part of keeping covenant, Mary and Joseph went to the temple for Mary's purification ritual after she gave birth. We read in Leviticus 12:2–8:

> "If a woman conceives and bears a male child, she shall be unclean seven days . . . the eighth day the flesh of his foreskin shall be circumcised. Her time of blood purification shall be thirty-three days. . . .
>
> When the days of her purification are completed, whether for a son or for a daughter, she shall bring to the priest at the entrance of the tent of meeting a lamb in its first year for a burnt offering and a pigeon or a turtledove for a purification offering. . . . If she cannot afford a sheep, she shall take two turtledoves or two pigeons, one for a burnt offering and the other for a purification offering, and the priest shall make atonement on her behalf, and she shall be clean."

Even though Luke's intended audience for the Gospel extended far beyond the Jewish community, Luke still wanted to establish that Mary and Joseph were faithful to Yahweh. They sought to follow the commands that their faith had set forth and did their best to fulfill them. Although they were too impoverished to afford a lamb as a sacrifice, they still purchased the two birds as Scripture ordered. In other words, Mary and Joseph were a faithful and righteous Jewish couple.

1. Today's symbols are turtle doves. What does the symbol mean in the context of today's Scripture reading?

2. How does the Holy Family's faithful practice of Judaism make the Gospel an extension of the stories from the Hebrew Scriptures?

3. In what ways do we show our faithfulness in the modern era? What are the outward signs of our inward commitment to God in our lives?

DECEMBER 29

Simeon
Luke 2:25–35

The Gospel of Luke begins with an emphasis on this being the continuation of an ancient story rather than the beginning of a new one. Luke followed in the literary footsteps of the writers of the Hebrew Scriptures and followed a similar route in how they framed the Hebrew prophets. Luke wrote the first two chapters of the Gospel to carefully establish that Jesus was set apart, with special circumstances around his birth and his first presentation at the temple.

Simeon prophesies that Jesus will serve as a light to the Gentiles in verse 32, serving as an extension of the promise that Abraham and Sarah were blessed so that "in you all the families of the earth shall be blessed" (Gen. 12:3). Jesus is to be a blessing for all the people of the earth.

In the temple scene, we encounter Simeon, whom God has promised to let see the Savior of Israel before his death. Simeon began with praise for God, thrilled that this day has arrived when Israel will be restored. However, we must keep in mind that the long-awaited and much-prophesied Savior for whom the people of Israel had waited was expected to lead the people triumphantly to war, conquering and expelling any occupying army or state. The people of Israel have not known complete autonomy and peace since the golden age of King David, and they longed to be restored to a similar circumstance. They were expecting a warrior to lead them to victory, not a weak and helpless infant who would grow into a teacher of love and peace.

Therefore, Simeon's ability to see Jesus' identity speaks greatly to Simeon's relationship with the Divine. Simeon's prophecy closely mirrored that of Isaiah 49:6: "I will give you as a light to the nations, that my salvation may reach to the end of the earth." Simeon understood the fate of this infant he held in his arms. But because he understood and had a vision of what was to come, he offered not a blessing but a grave word of warning to Mary: "and a sword will pierce your own soul, too" (Luke 2:35). Later in the Gospels, we witness Mary watching as her firstborn son died on a cross and lived into this dire prophecy of Simeon.

As humans, we tend to be afraid of the night because we are diurnal, which means we evolved to operate in the daylight and sleep when it is dark outside. This is the opposite of animals who are nocturnal and active at night, like owls, fireflies, bats, and coyotes. These animals are designed to sleep during the day. Night offers rest and relief from the obligations of work in a world without artificial light.

But humans like to see our surroundings, and our eyesight

is not well adapted for seeing in the dark. When a strange noise wakes you up in the middle of the night, what is your first instinct? For most people, the first reaction is to turn on a light, whether that's turning on a lamp or grabbing a cell phone or flashlight. Obviously, some sort of fire, like a candle, would have been used before the invention of electricity, and so today's symbol of a candle is meant to represent the light that Simeon references. A light when we are frightened in the dark is like a breath of fresh air. This is how much the hope Christ brings into the world means for God's people.

1. Today's symbol is a candle. What does the symbol mean in the context of today's Scripture reading?

2. After dark, find a flashlight and some time to play. Remember how much fun a flashlight used to be when you were a kid? Recreate that experience today and remember how comforting it could be to know that there was a flashlight within arm's reach in the dark.

3. What were the people around Simeon expecting when they spoke of a savior for Israel? How did Jesus live into these expectations, and in what ways did Jesus defy these expectations?

DECEMBER 30

Anna
Luke 2:36–40

As a United Methodist pastor, I serve in an itinerant system. Every year, I submit a form that says if I want to stay serving my current church(es), want to be moved, or am somewhere in between. My church leaders fill out a similar form, expressing their wishes. My supervisors then decide where my gifts and graces are most needed within the geographical boundaries of my Annual Conference (in my case, the states of Kansas and Nebraska).

When I arrive in a new church, my years of experience have taught me that I should immediately begin to study and learn. I try to understand the dynamics of the community surrounding the church, how the church currently operates, and who holds key leadership positions, and I always look for the matriarch. She may or may not hold a designated leadership position. However, she has historically been easy to find: I go into the kitchen at the first big church event and observe who is creating order in the chaos of food preparation.

While the remaining records of the temple in Jerusalem make it seem unlikely that there was a large kitchen on the premises, when I regard Anna the prophetess, I still regard her as the matriarch at the temple. In the strictly patriarchal setting of ancient Judaism, there were entire sections of the temple in Jerusalem that women were not allowed to enter. Anna had been a childless widow for the majority of her life, meaning that in her culture, she lived the majority of her life without financial support or security. Despite these restrictions and oppressions, she still opened herself up to become a prophet, a megaphone for the Divine.

While Anna's prophecy is not recorded, we know that she was elated at meeting the Holy Family. Anna dedicated her life to prayer at the temple, most likely living off charitable contributions from religious pilgrims to the temple. She rejoiced that she had lived to see this day and celebrated that the redemption of Israel was at hand. The salvation of her people had finally come!

Today's symbol is a scroll. In the ancient world, the

Hebrew Scriptures were kept on scrolls carefully copied from one generation to the next by Hebrew scribes, and frequently prophets wrote down their revelations on scrolls. There are no scrolls mentioned in today's text, so this may seem like an odd symbol to most Protestants. However, within both the Roman Catholic as well as the Eastern Orthodox traditions, there are many depictions of Anna the prophetess. The majority of iconography depicting Anna depicts her with either a rolled or an unrolled scroll in one hand. Artists throughout the ages have drawn her with a scroll in her hand to represent her place within the prophetic tradition.

1. Today's symbol is a scroll. What does the symbol mean in the context of today's Scripture reading?

2. Name the church matriarchs that you have known. Who were the quiet yet powerful matriarchs? Who were the ones consistently in charge?

3. Christian traditions that ordain female clergy are recent developments in the broader history of the church. Yet matriarchs have always held positions of power in our churches. How have women gifted with leadership found ways to lead throughout the history of the church, even in traditions that deny their gifts?

DECEMBER 31

The Shema
Deuteronomy 6:1–8

Growing up, I had a number of Jewish friends, and sometimes I went over to their houses when we played together. While waiting at the door after ringing the bell, I began to notice that all my Jewish friends' homes had a similar small piece of metal attached to the doorframes on the front doors. Although I asked several friends what they were, kids tended to reply simply: "it's just a thing we do." Finally, I received a substantive answer in high school when one friend finally told me that it was a *mezuzah* and that there was a tiny scroll sealed inside. He told me that it was a sort of blessing for their house. I later learned that most Jewish people, even many who consider themselves only culturally Jewish (meaning they acknowledge their heritage but don't necessarily attend synagogue or believe the tenets of Judaism), will still hang a *mezuzah* on the front door of their homes.

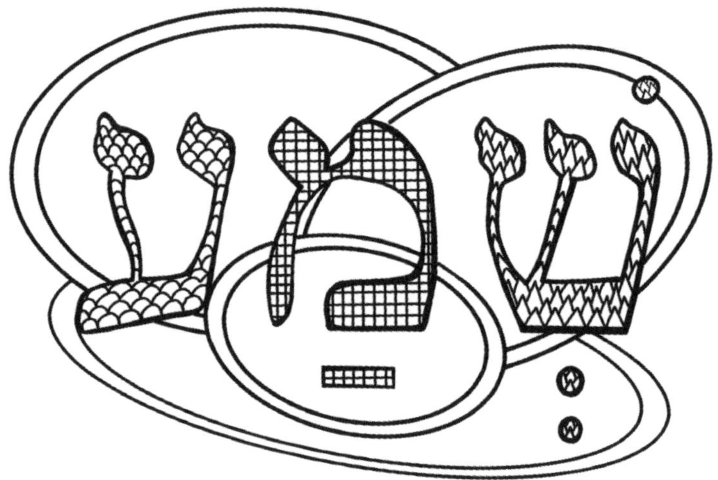

A *mezuzah* doesn't contain just any scroll, however. It contains a small slip of parchment bearing the words of the *Shema*, a Hebrew prayer we find in today's Scripture reading. The first word of today's Scripture reading in Hebrew is *shema*, which means "hear!" or "listen!" Thus, over time, this passage has come to be known simply as "the *shema*." "Hear, O Israel: The Lord is our God, the Lord alone. You shall love the Lord your God with all your heart and with all your soul and with all your might" (Deut 6:4-5). This is a prayer that Jewish people still use to this day. The rabbis commanded reciting the Shema twice a day—once when the people arose and once before bed at night. We might think of this as Judaism's version of a prayer that even children are expected to recite.

Unsurprisingly, as Jesus practiced Judaism, we find reference to the Shema in the New Testament. When Jesus was asked, "What is the greatest commandment?" in all three Synoptic Gospels (Matthew, Mark, and Luke), his answer was twofold: "Love the Lord your God with all your heart, soul, mind, and strength, and love your neighbor as yourself." For the first part of his response, he drew directly from the Shema, a prayer that would be well known to every Jewish person in the audience.

The Shema makes clear that God's primary commandment is love, not fear, obedience, or sacrifice. Keep your souls focused toward God first and foremost, and love God with all that you are. This does not mean this is the only thing God requires of us, but it is the first and foremost command.

At the heart of nearly every story in Scripture we find the core message: love God and love your neighbor as yourself. Although I love the stories of the Bible and am a lifelong student of the text, the themes found in Scripture keep repeating themselves. Human beings keep making the same mistakes over and over again. We need the rest of the Bible because we are not so good at loving God first and foremost, and we are terrible at loving our neighbors, and often we are not good at loving ourselves. I firmly believe the rest of Scripture largely exists to inform us how to do this basic and simple task—the most simple, fundamental, and, ironically, the most complicated commandment that Scripture contains for human beings: love God and love one another.

1. Today's symbol is the word *shema* in Hebrew script. What does the symbol mean in the context of today's Scripture reading?

2. Why is the Shema a prayer Jewish people are taught to repeat multiple times a day, every day of their lives?

What does this prayer teach, and how does this prayer instruct?

3. In what ways do you find loving God with all your heart, soul, mind, and strength to be an easy task? In what ways do you find that this commandment takes everything you have to follow it?

JANUARY 1

Grafted Branches
Romans 11:13–24

While some religions tend toward evangelism—the practice of seeking out and recruiting new members—Judaism has never been a faith that encourages evangelism at all. Due to the lack of evangelistic tendencies, although people can choose to convert to Judaism, in both the ancient and modern world, the most common way a person becomes Jewish is being born into Judaism.

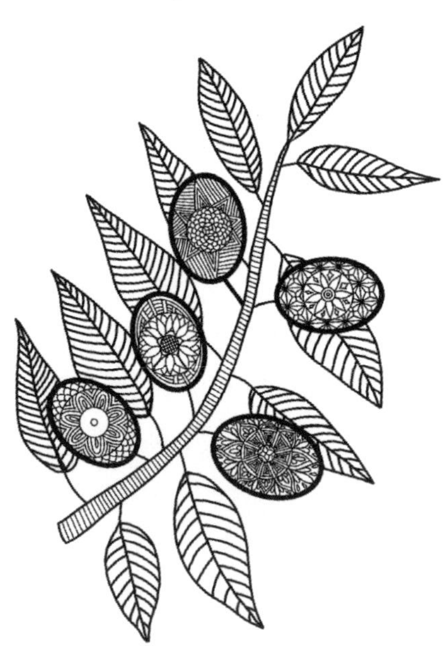

For the past fifteen hundred years, Judaism has been tracked through the maternal line. This might seem odd to anyone who has paid close attention to Scripture, as in both the Hebrew text and New Testament, families were repeatedly traced through the paternal lines. It was extremely rare for women to even be mentioned in long lists of the ancestors. Scholars argue about when and why the Jewish community shifted and began tracking Judaism through the mother's line, but the shift clearly began around fifteen hundred years ago. Therefore, for the past fifteen centuries, a person has been considered Jewish if their mother was Jewish and a Gentile if she was not.

Thus, only people with Jewish mothers are born into the covenant that God established with Abraham and Sarah; the majority of Christian people qualify as Gentiles—outside of the family of Abraham and Sarah. Today's Scripture explains that through Jesus Christ, Gentiles may also be a part of the family of Abraham and Sarah by being grafted onto the branches of the roots of Judaism.

Grafting is an agricultural process whereby an ideal plant is attached to an ideal root system. The branch of a healthy plant of one variety is cut and attached to an opened section of the stem of the desired root system from another variety of plant. The two are then bandaged together, resulting in something that looks quite similar to a human limb being wrapped in a modern-day elastic bandage.

In both the ancient and modern world, this is a common practice with grape vines, olive trees, and fruit trees. And in the modern era, many gardeners practice grafting with their tomato plants. Grafting became prevalent because it is common for one variety of plant to have a strong root system but produce small or undesirable fruit. It is also common for a plant variety that produces desirable fruit to have an inadequate or weak root system. Grafting allows the farmer to take advantage of one variety's strong root system while simultaneously taking advantage of another variety's excellent fruit production. In the modern world, it is also common to graft fruit trees together for planting in confined spaces—making one plant capable of cross-pollinating with itself by having two different varieties growing from the same root system.

The metaphor of grafting branches is used in this passage, meaning that the children of Abraham are the original root system—those who are Jewish by birth and by heritage. Those who are not Jewish have been grafted into the family—attached through Jesus to the greater, preexisting root structure. Christians consider themselves adopted children into the family of Abraham. Just as we learn stories from our families that took place before we were born, these stories contribute to who we are. Human beings are made up of stories that were told long before our own existence. In the same way, Christians are a part of a larger ongoing story of the Divine—one that begins in Genesis and continues far into the future. We have been grafted into God's greater ongoing story.

1. Today's symbol is an olive branch. What does the symbol mean in the context of today's Scripture reading?

2. Did you already know about the practice of grafting? What does it mean that most Christians are not born but grafted into the family of Abraham?

3. In light of this metaphor, list some ways in which studying the stories of the Hebrew Scriptures is a vital foundation for Christians.

JANUARY 2

Adopted into the Family
Romans 8:12–17

Today's symbol is an image of a child's handprint inside a parent's handprint, representing the text's theme of adoption. In the Disney movie *Lilo and Stitch*, a little girl named Lilo adopts what she believes is a stray puppy and names him Stitch. It turns out Stitch is actually an alien from another planet who is trying to escape from his own people. Against all odds, Lilo, her older sister, Nani, and Stitch come together to form a family. Throughout the movie, Lilo often says, "Family means no one gets left behind or forgotten."[7]

Families come in all shapes and sizes; people can become family members in all sorts of ways. Sometimes family members are related by genetics and are mirror images of one another. One day during my childhood, I came down the stairs and was confused by a picture that sat on top of a pile of papers. It looked like a school picture of my little sister, but it was in black and white, so I took the photograph to my mom to ask why. She laughed when I asked the question: "Why is this picture of Kelli in black and white?" It wasn't a photo of my sister at all. It was a picture of my mom as a little girl. I was shocked, and as I examined the photo more closely, I could see a few features that my sister does not have. But the family resemblance was like a mirror image from one generation to the next.

However, not all family members are related by DNA. Sometimes people are adopted into a family, sometimes family members are related through marriage, and sometimes we have people that we choose to consider part of our families. Christians have been adopted into God's family tree; we are not strangers or outsiders in God's realm but counted as beloved family. Through the spirit of baptism, Christians put on Christ and are welcomed into the family of God. It is vital to our understanding of Christianity to diligently study our sacred texts in their entirety, because we are called to understand the heritage of the family we have joined.

But adoption is not a singular event—it impacts the entire future of a family unit. Because our families are formed and changed every time a new family member is added, family itself is an ongoing work in progress. In the same way, the Christian family is an ongoing work in progress. With each new member adopted through their baptism, the family grows and changes.

The celebration of Christmas represents God's inbreak into the world, the moment when there is a shift in the story of God and God's people. Through our adoption through Jesus Christ, the family of God is opened up to all the nations of the earth rather than limited to the bloodlines of Abraham and Sarah. The family of God is multiplied by this new inbreak into the world.

1. Today's symbol is two handprints. What does the symbol mean in the context of today's Scripture reading?

2. What does it mean to be adopted into God's family? How is this metaphor employed in today's Scripture? How does the metaphor of grafting continue to apply within the context of today's text?

3. Think about people you consider family despite sharing zero DNA. They might be family through marriage, adoption, or even chosen family who are not related to you in any legally recognized sense. Describe the importance of these people to your concept of family.

JANUARY 3

Grafted into the Family Tree
Romans 15:7–13

Our symbol today carries on the metaphor of grafting and growth by depicting a tree budding in spring. We continue to explore the themes of Gentiles having been grafted onto the family tree of Abraham.

Early in my ministry, I received a phone call from a parent one Monday morning. I had been teaching confirmation class to a group of seventh graders the day before, and the curriculum we were using had us read today's Scripture passage aloud. One of the girls raised her hand and innocently asked, "What is circumcision?" After a lot of snickering from all the boys and a few of the girls in the room, I answered her question. At least, I thought I did.

The confused parent asked on that Monday morning, "Did you teach the class that when a Jewish boy is eight days old, his parents cut off his penis?" I responded that I had not, that I had said that they cut the foreskin away from the penis—but by that time, the embarrassed twelve-year-old was apparently only absorbing every other word. I most likely failed to offer a full anatomical description of foreskin, which muddied the waters.

The religious value of circumcision, however, can be unclear even for those who understand the procedure. In that region at that point in history, only Jewish males were circumcised—and since the Jesus movement was still considered a sect of Judaism, some argued that Gentile Christian men must also follow Jewish practice and be circumcised. These early Christians still did not understand that they were forming an entirely new religious movement; for several centuries, most people (including Christians themselves) still considered people following Jesus to be a Jewish sect. Paul argued throughout his letters, however, that Gentiles did not have to become Jewish to follow Jesus.

Paul makes his case in today's reading by quoting the Hebrew Scriptures: Psalm 18:49, Deuteronomy 32:43, Psalm 117:1, and Isaiah 11:10. Today's Scripture helps to bring us full circle from where we began Advent devotions together. In Genesis 22, we saw the promise that God made that Sarah and Abraham would be blessed to be a blessing to all the nations of the earth: "and by your offspring shall all the nations of the earth gain blessing for themselves, because you have obeyed my voice" (v. 18). Jesus' presence in the world is a way in which God extends that blessing beyond the realm of Judaism, and the good news extends to the Gentiles through this spirit of adoption through Christ.

And by quoting Isaiah, Paul once more brings us back to the stump of the tree of Jesse. "The root of Jesse shall come, the one who rises to rule the gentiles; in him the gentiles shall hope" (Rom. 15:12). Through the faithfulness of Abraham and Sarah, and those embedded in their story throughout the ages, and through the offspring of Jesse down to the birth of Jesus, the promised blessing has extended to all the nations of the earth.

1. Today's symbol is a budding branch. What does the symbol mean in the context of today's Scripture reading?

2. The apostle Paul brings up circumcision in several different letters we find in the New Testament. Why was Paul so concerned with the practice of circumcision given what you now know about the cultural context of the time?

3. How does today's Scripture help to bring us full circle in our Advent study? Spend some time in reflection, and name some moments of insight that you have experienced in spending this time with our sacred text.

JANUARY 4

Love
Matthew 22:34–40

Full confession: I dislike most fictional stories that center on romance. The two people the story creators want together are frequently caught in complicated situations simply because they are emotionally immature and have poor communication skills. I understand if we were to tell the story of two fully actualized human beings with strong communication skills, there is unlikely to be much story worth the time it takes to tell it. That said, I find most "love stories" to be problematic.

In today's text, the Pharisees are trying to catch Jesus in a statement of heresy by forcing him to choose the most important of the commandments. Instead, Jesus turns the entire episode on its head by speaking of the greatest love story ever told. Jesus gives them an unexpected answer, one with which they have no theological framework to argue.

The Shema, "Love the Lord your God with all your heart, soul, mind, and strength," is inherently fundamental to Jewish belief, both in Jesus' era as well as within our own. But the second part of this golden rule does not feel so far removed from the first. First of all, there is an assumption in this passage that people will love themselves. Most folks don't do well at following this second command, but for different reasons. Some people are really good at loving themselves and struggle to love others and empathize with the experiences of other human beings. Others are incredibly skilled and talented at loving other people but frequently neglect the art of loving oneself, often putting their own physical, mental, and spiritual needs on the back burner of their lives. We either tend toward too much self-love or not enough. We are called to a happy medium between these two extremes, but we seem to desperately struggle to find balance and fulfill this commandment to "love others as ourselves."

The Greek word for love in this instance is *agape*. In the time Scripture was written, there were multiple words for love in Koine Greek. We use *love* quite flippantly in the English language; I will say both "I love ice cream" and "I love my husband," although clearly my love looks quite different in these two circumstances. Koine Greek had some clarification for this by having different words for different types of love, including godly love, romantic love, brotherly/friendship love, familial love, practical love, and more.

When we read the story of creation a few weeks ago, we established that humankind was created in God's divine image. It does not seem like a stretch from this understanding that loving God also means loving our fellow human beings, and loving our fellow human beings and loving ourselves are a part of caring for God's phenomenal creation. If all people are created in God's image, then all people must be loved and cared for, as reflections of the divine image that they are. Loving our neighbors as ourselves does not seem a great stretch from the first commandment, in that all our neighbors have been created in the image of the Divine. Loving our neighbor is akin to loving God in such a manner. Loving ourselves is akin to loving God in such a manner.

Through Jesus, we are invited to be participants in God's ongoing story of love. This is a love story that I can buy into, with every ounce of my heart and soul. Rather than a story of deceit and miscommunication, this is the original story of what it means to be called to love—the true *agape* love of the Divine.

1. Today's symbol is a heart. What does the symbol mean in the context of today's Scripture reading?

2. How does the precision of the Koine Greek words for *love* help you think through how we use the word in English? How does the use of *agape* influence how we might think of the love of God?

3. Which group do you tend to fall into? Loving yourself too much and struggling with empathy, or loving others too much and neglecting yourself? In what ways have you fought against your instincts in an attempt to reach the balance required by God's call to love?

4. How does this text inform our basic understanding of love, and what might it look like to offer that love in our world?

JANUARY 5

Journey of the Magi
Matthew 2:1–6

Today is the twelfth day of Christmas, the day before Epiphany when we celebrate the magi's visit to the Holy Family. When I was in college, during Advent my campus minister would unpack his own personal nativity scene and display it in a public area of the campus ministry house. But in attempts to be more faithful to scriptural renderings, he set up his Christmas decor in an unusual way. First, baby Jesus was never added to the manger until December 25. He would hide the Jesus figurine in his own apartment until Christmas Day. Second, he put the magi across the room from the rest of the manger scene—to make clear to us that the magi should still be traveling and only arrive at Epiphany on January 6. I began to learn that many of my perceptions of the Christmas story were far more cultural than biblical.

First, let's look at the word used to describe the magi. The original text in Koine Greek uses *magoi*, the plural of *magos*. *Magos* typically referred to a member of the priestly caste of ancient Persia, where most people practiced Zoroastrianism. Although Western culture typically depicts three magi, often there are twelve magi depicted in the Eastern church (such as the Orthodox traditions)—

neither number is inherently correct or incorrect; we know only that there was more than one (because *magoi* is plural) and that there were three gifts given. There are no other numbers offered up. The Western church typically depicts three magi because of the three gifts.

The magi are also often depicted riding camels. Our symbol for today is a camel. While a camel or camels would have been the most likely means of transportation across a desert for the magi's caravan, this detail is not mentioned in the text—we are not certain how they traveled.

Furthermore, they visit Jesus in a house, implying that Jesus has been moved from the manger at the scene of his birth. And it is entirely possible that they do not arrive until Jesus is old enough to be weaned and walking, especially since Herod orders all males under the age of two to be slaughtered.

Herod is frightened when he hears the magi speak of the "king of the Jews" because Herod knows his own rule is tenuous. Although Herod claimed to practice Judaism, his reign was one of terror and violence. His title, "king of the Jews," was granted by the Roman Empire, but no one lived under any illusions that Herod was a servant of the Jewish people. He functioned as a puppet for the Roman Empire, outwardly claiming to justly rule his Jewish subjects but in fact acting as a self-serving pawn of Rome. Herod lived in the shadow of fear as all tyrants do, terrified that someone would rise up and take away his tenuous hold on power. This is why Herod is so disturbed by the idea that someone else might receive the title "king of the Jews," even if that someone is a helpless infant.

His panic grew when the priests and scribes he consulted read Micah's prophecy saying that from Bethlehem "shall come a ruler" who was to lead Israel (Matt. 2:6, referencing Micah 5:2). The book of Micah rotates between oracles of judgment and oracles of restoration, and this particular quote is from an oracle of restoration, offering the people hope in the midst of destruction. Like the people of Micah's time, fearing invasion by Assyria and Babylon, the Jewish people of Herod's time were living in constant fear under Roman occupation, and the prophecy in Micah applied as much to them in the time of Jesus as it did when the words were first written. The magi unintentionally created a stir by upsetting an unstable tyrant at a time when the political environment was already fraught with tension.

The magi at the beginning of Matthew's story represent that the broader story of the Divine is being opened wide for all the peoples of the earth. These foreign visitors represent the widening of God's kin-dom from the beginning of Jesus' story, a theme that carries on into the present, and into the future when Jesus returns.

1. Today's symbol is a camel. What does the symbol mean in the context of today's Scripture reading?

2. Why was Herod so upset to hear the magi refer to someone else as the "king of the Jews"? Tyrants throughout history have tended to be people who are unstable; why do you think these people are drawn to power, and what about their tenuous grip on power makes them so paranoid?

3. What did you learn in today's reflection about magi that you might not have known before?

JANUARY 6 (EPIPHANY)

Magi Visit Jesus
Matthew 2:7–15

Across Jesus' infancy narratives in Matthew and Luke, the magi are the only Gentiles to visit baby Jesus. While the visit of the shepherds in Luke signifies that Jesus has been sent not just for the elite but for all classes and castes of human society, the visit of the magi marks that Jesus has not just been sent for the Jewish people. This harkens back to the original promise that God made when establishing the covenant with Abraham and Sarah, that by their "offspring shall all the nations of the earth gain blessing for themselves" (Gen. 22:18).

The magi received word in a dream to disobey Herod's orders. They took a great risk in failing to follow his instructions—not only because he was the ruler of the region but also because he was a well-known merciless tyrant. (He did not hesitate to put his own son and wife to death to protect his own position.) But the magi, as the wise people the Scripture names them to be, simply took another road to avoid Herod altogether. Herod's reach did not extend far beyond his small piece of the world, and they were safe soon after they left his territory.

Matthew put a great deal of importance on dreams. This is not surprising, as interpreting dreams as divine messages was common practice across the cultures of the region. Ancient documentation has been recovered regarding dream interpretation from the Ancient Egyptians, Mesopotamians, Greeks,

Romans, Assyrians, and more. Joseph was told in a dream that Mary's child is from the Holy Spirit and that Joseph should marry her and raise the child. The magi were warned in a dream to leave by a path that avoided Herod, and then Joseph was also warned in a dream to flee with Mary and Jesus into Egypt to escape Herod's wrath.

This story is told as the anti-exodus, a turning of events in which Egypt is a place of safety rather than a place of slavery. Furthermore, as Joseph and Mary fled with their child, they became immigrants, refugees, and foreigners in a foreign land. They were attempting to escape from religious persecution by fleeing into another country, which is the fundamental definition of a refugee.

Many years ago, after preaching on this passage, I had a parishioner confront me, angrily informing me that her "Lord and Savior was not a refugee!" She refused to engage in further conversation, but her comment made me suspect that she carried some strong misconceptions about the nature of people who are labeled immigrants and refugees. Immigrants and refugees have, throughout earth's history, frequently encountered xenophobia and racism; the United States has not been an exception to this trend. It is easier to see such people as a problem to be solved or sent away rather than to remember that those who have fled in fear for their own lives and their children's lives are also beloved children of God. If every person viewed refugee families with their children as though they might be the Holy Family in disguise, how would our culture be forced to reckon with its previously held assumptions and biases?

Today we celebrate Epiphany, recognizing that *epiphany* is a word defined as "sudden revelation" or "sudden understanding." An epiphany is that moment when you have been feeling confused and unclear, and suddenly everything becomes clear in a moment of: "Oh! Now I get it!" Because I believe that faith is a journey, part of an ongoing story, I don't believe that Christians have one magical moment where everything makes sense within the confines of our present existence. However, I hope and pray that you have had a few of those moments as we have journeyed together—exploring the hope that can be found in the living roots of Jesse's tree, in the story of Jesus in the manger, and in the story that you carry with you as you go forth into the world and continue to carry on the love story of the Divine.

1. Today's symbol is a star. What does the symbol mean in the context of today's Scripture reading?

2. What does it mean that the Holy Family fled into Egypt as refugees? What does this say about how God approaches people who are fleeing for their lives from the dangers at home?

3. How does the visit of the magi continue to open up the incarnation of Jesus to the Gentiles? Why is their presence in the story significant in this regard? How will you carry the incarnation of Jesus in your heart all year long?

Family Devotions

I have worked with a lot of kids over the years and frequently see families who are not traditional families, for many different reasons. When I speak to kids, I refer to their guardians as "your grown-ups," knowing full well that not all children I work with have family settings in which they live with their biological parents. I have done this throughout these devotions as well. If it works for your family, you are welcome to substitute *parents* for *grown-ups*. However, I have found that even with children from traditional family settings, "your grown-ups" opens up a question to the entire community of adults in their lives (teachers, grandparents, aunts, uncles, family friends, etc.).

I encourage you to use an old-school printed version of a Bible when you read the Scripture passages to the kids. If you don't have one, an app on your phone will work just fine. But there is something official about sitting down with the actual book that gives a different weight to doing the study.

"Repeat-after-Me Prayers" are something I have learned to use with the kids I serve in my churches. These prayers help teach children how to pray by offering them words to use and letting them own the words as their own. They are also excellent tools for kids who have not yet learned how to read or who struggle with reading. After saying "This is a repeat-after-me prayer!" give everyone some time to start repeating after you. I have written them in an almost poetic format with very short lines, making sure that the lines are easy to repeat.

If you have children who are old enough, consider having them read the Scripture for the day. If they are not yet old enough, let them color the symbol for the day while you read the Scripture. This way, they are still participants and not just sitting still while you read the Scripture.

These devotions will cover an abridged version of the forty-day experience written for adults. There are twelve devotions in total: two for each of the four weeks of Advent, and then one each for Christmas Eve, Christmas Day, the Sunday after Christmas, and Epiphany. These devotionals attempt to cover similar themes as the longer readings but are written with a younger audience in mind.

FIRST SUNDAY OF ADVENT

A Branch of the Tree of Jesse
Isaiah 11:1–9

In the church, the season of Christmas doesn't start until Christmas Day. There is an entire season called Advent that begins four weeks before the excitement of Christmas Day. For the next four weeks, Christians remember who we are and who Jesus is, and we remember that our faith asks us to love God and to love other people. And *then* we will celebrate Jesus' birthday! Waiting can be difficult, but we can all join in and wait together. We are going to journey together through the season of Advent to get ready for Christmas in our hearts.

Have you ever heard of a family tree? It is a record of our ancestors: our parents, grandparents, great-grandparents, and so on. It's called a tree because when a family tree is drawn on paper, all the lines make it look like the branches of a tree.

In the next few weeks, we will look at Jesus' family tree and some of the stories that happened before Jesus came into the world. Have a grown-up show you how much of a Bible is the Old Testament. There are a lot of stories in the Bible before Jesus is born!

For many types of trees, if a tree has a strong root system, the tree will slowly grow back if it is cut down and the root system is left intact. A tree shoot will begin to grow out of the stump. The prophet Isaiah is using a metaphor in our Scripture today, which means he is using an image to represent an idea about the ancient nation of Israel. At this point, Israel was in danger from other countries, and it looked as if their army was going to be defeated. The prophet Isaiah is comparing the family of the beloved King David to a tree by reminding us that when a tree is chopped down, it doesn't always mean the tree is dead—there is often new life within the roots of the tree. In the same way, even though it looks as if the family tree of King David and his father, Jesse, has come to an end, there is still hope for God's people.

As Christians, this is important for us because King David becomes one of Jesus' ancestors; David shows up in Jesus' family tree! During the next few weeks, we will celebrate the hope found in today's Scripture as we wait for Christmas Day. Eventually, on Christmas Day, we will join together to celebrate the hope that Christians find in the birth of Jesus.

Reflection Questions

1. Today's symbol is a tree stump. Why is this the symbol for today? What does it mean?

2. Ask your grown-ups to help you draw a family tree for your family. Who do you know in the family tree? Are there people you never got to meet? Ask your grown-ups to tell you some stories about the people in the drawing whom you never met. How are these people still a part of your story?

3. What is the season of Advent? How is it different from the Christmas season?

4. What do you think it means to have hope? How might this be a season of hope for Christian people?

Repeat-after-Me Prayer

This is a repeat-after-me prayer!

Dear God,
we give you thanks
for all the stories
that make us who we are.
We give you thanks
for our own family tree,
and we give you thanks
for Jesus' family tree.
Help us to prepare
for the coming of Christmas
through the season of Advent.
Amen.

FIRST WEEK OF ADVENT

Samuel Anoints David
1 Samuel 16:1–13

Oftentimes, grown-ups will ask kids not to do certain things because they are trying to keep the kids safe and healthy. But every once in a while, grown-ups just forget how capable kids can be. Have you ever been underestimated because you were too young or too little? In our Bible story today, we meet someone whom God chose even though all the people around him believed he was too young and too little.

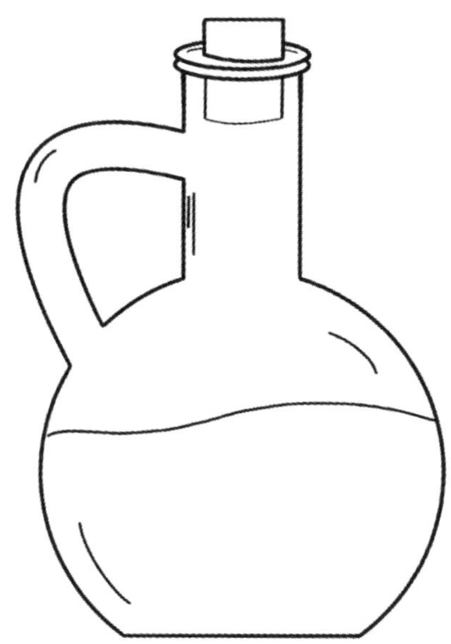

Ancient Israel's first king—King Saul—wasn't doing a very good job. Unlike in a democracy, the people of Israel couldn't simply elect a new leader. So God sent the prophet Samuel to choose a new king by anointing, which meant pouring out olive oil over a person's head. Even in our modern world, it takes thousands of olives to make enough olive oil to fill your hands cupped together. In the ancient world, without machines and electricity, olive oil was a very expensive substance because it took so much effort to make it. The Israelites poured out such an expensive item to show the importance of the king; when Samuel anointed David, he declared for everyone present that David was a very important person.

God tells the prophet Samuel that the new king will be one of Jesse's sons. Samuel goes to Jesse's house and asks him to bring out all his sons. Jesse understands how important this is, so he calls all his sons—except the youngest—to stand in a line in front of Samuel. God tells Samuel that none of these young men are going to be the next king. Jesse hadn't even thought to bring his youngest son in from taking care of the sheep in the fields because he was so certain that God would not be interested in choosing such a young boy.

In those days, a king was expected to lead the army into battle if the country needed to go to war. This meant that everyone was looking for a strong and mighty warrior, not a small kid who watched his family's flock of sheep. Everyone, even Samuel, is shocked that God has chosen David to be the next king of Israel.

As Christian people, we are currently celebrating the season of Advent, a time when we prepare our hearts and minds for the birth of Jesus Christ. During this season of waiting, we remember that God took on human form and came into the world as Jesus in Bethlehem. We know that King David was able to change his country even when he was very young—but through his birth, Jesus changed the entire world as a baby! If a baby can create this much change, consider how you can also remind people that they are loved by God as we continue to prepare for Christmas.

Reflection Questions

1. Today's symbol is an oil flask. An oil flask is an ancient container for oil, but its contents were similar to the olive oil that you can buy at the grocery store. Why is this the symbol for today? What does it mean?

2. What does it feel like to be underestimated because you are too young or too little? How does it make you feel that God chose David to be king, even though everyone else (even his own father!) thought he was way too young and little? What does this teach us about who God chooses for God's team?

3. Why is everyone surprised when David is chosen to be king?

4. How can we look at who people are on the inside, the way that God does, instead of making judgments about how people look on the outside?

Repeat-after-Me Prayer

This is a repeat-after-me prayer!

Dear God,
we give you thanks
that you see us
for who we are.
Help us to see
other people
as you see them
and to remember that all people
are created in your image.
Amen.

SECOND SUNDAY OF ADVENT

Prince of Peace
Isaiah 9:2–7

Have you ever been afraid of the dark? The dark can be very scary for human beings, especially because we are diurnal, which means we are awake in the daylight and sleep when it is dark outside. This is the opposite of animals who are nocturnal and active at night, like owls, fireflies, bats, and coyotes. These animals are designed to sleep during the day. We like to see our surroundings, but our eyesight is not well adapted for seeing in the dark. One of the ways we cope with this is by using artificial light once the sun goes down; we turn on a lamp or use a flashlight.

In the time of the Bible, people did not have electricity. This means that they could not just turn on a light with the flip of a switch. Their lamps involved using a small fire as their source of light. When you see the image for today's symbol, it might remind you of the type of lamp that a genie would come out of rather than the lamp that is next to your bed at night. That's because this is how a lot of lamps looked in the ancient world, instead of what we have today.

In our Scripture for today, the prophet Isaiah, in the form of poetry, is using another metaphor—an image to illustrate a complex idea. At the time Isaiah is writing, long ago, the people of the country Israel were very scared that they were going to lose their homes and their independence. There were a lot of countries with stronger armies who were threatening their borders, and they were afraid. Isaiah's metaphor is that the frightened people are like people living in the dark, and he explains that this prophecy promises that there is hope of light in their future.

Sometimes when we are very sad or afraid, we worry that we are never going to feel better. This is how the people of Israel were feeling, as if they were never going to feel better. The prophet Isaiah was promising that God would not let them feel this sad and afraid forever—that eventually things were going to get better. Sometimes when we are having a bad day or week, we also feel as if things are never going to get better. God promises us that even though we might feel sad or afraid, God is always with us.

Today's story reminds us that God can serve as our light in the dark, and as we continue our journey to Christmas, we know that the birth of Jesus also served as a light in the darkness. Jesus was born at a time when things were very bad for his people—they were treated very poorly by people of another country who were controlling their country. When Jesus comes into the world, his people are in need of hope—and the hope of Jesus is still present with us today!

Reflection Questions

1. Today's symbol is an ancient lamp. Why is a lamp the symbol for today? What does it mean?

2. Can you tell a story about a time when you were afraid of the dark? What made you feel better? How did the story end? How might you remind yourself that God is with you when you are afraid?

3. When the people of Israel are feeling sad and afraid, God assures them that things will get better. God also makes this promise to us. Can you name a time when you had a bad day and then things got better? God was with you, even when things weren't going well!

4. After it is dark outside, ask your grown-ups to turn off the lights in a room and let you play with a flashlight. How do things look different in the dark? How does it make you feel to know you have the light in your hands? Even when we can't see God, God is still with us, just like the comfort we feel while holding a flashlight in the dark.

Repeat-after-Me Prayer

This is a repeat-after-me prayer!

Dear God,
we give you thanks
that we are never alone
because you are always with us!
Help us to remember
to turn to you
when we are afraid or sad
and to remember
that you never leave us.
Amen.

SECOND WEEK OF ADVENT

Creation

Genesis 1:1–2:3

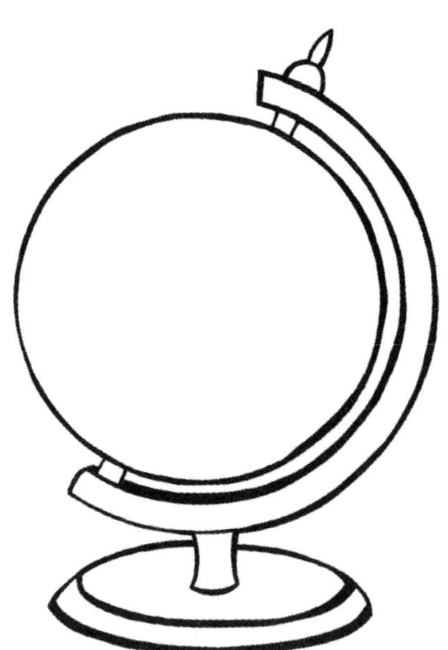

Have you ever been incredibly proud of something that you made? Maybe it was a drawing or a sculpture, or maybe you helped an adult bake something that tasted incredible. After you finished your creation, what did you want to do? I'm betting you wanted to show off your work to people you love and have them see your amazing creation.

Just like when you make something you are proud of, God was proud when God made everything in creation. God made the whole world and everything in it, from the tiniest ladybug to the blue whale! Every leaf you see, every animal you encounter, every person you meet, they are all a part of God's creation. In the story we read today, God created all the things in our world. Then, when God saw all the things God had made, God shouted, "Woah! This is so awesome!"

And the best part of this story? God said that even after making human beings.

Even though it feels as if Christmas is all around us, we are still in the season of Advent, a season when we are preparing and waiting for Christmas. As we continue to wait for Jesus' birthday, we know that Jesus' greatest command was that we love God and we love other people as we love ourselves. When God made you, God stood back and said, "Woah! This is so awesome!" Every person you will ever meet is created in the image of God, which means that we are all children of God. How might that impact how we treat the world around us, how we treat other people, and even how we treat ourselves?

Reflection Questions

1. Today's symbol is a globe. Why do you think that is the symbol for the day? What does it mean?

2. Name a time when you created something that made you really proud. What was it, and can you describe how you felt when you showed it to other people?

3. Name five things from the natural world that make you say "Woah!" Why do you find these things so interesting?

4. From your eyelashes to the farthest star, God made everything, and everything was good. Can you name some good traits that you have? Can you name some good traits that the other people in your home have?

How might these traits be reflections of the God who created us all?

Repeat-after Me Prayer

This is a repeat-after-me prayer!

Dear God,
we give you thanks
for what you have created.
We give you thanks
that all people are created in your image—
including me!
Help me remember to give thanks
for all the beautiful things in this world,
which also includes me!
Amen.

THIRD SUNDAY OF ADVENT

Ruth
Ruth 1:1–22

In the movie *Lilo and Stitch*, a little girl named Lilo adopts what she believes is a puppy and names him Stitch. It turns out Stitch is actually an alien from another planet who is trying to escape from his own people. Against all odds, Lilo, her older sister, Nani, and Stitch come together to form a family. Throughout the movie, Lilo often says, "Family means no one gets left behind or forgotten." Stitch adds to this sentiment: "This is my family. I found it, all on my own. It's little, and broken, but still good. Yeah, still good."[8]

Families come in all shapes and sizes, and we can consider some people family members in all sorts of ways. Sometimes family members are related by genetics, which also is called DNA. When family members are related in this way, they might look like each other. For example, when I go somewhere with my mom and my sister, everyone immediately knows we are related because we look so much alike.

However, not all family members are related by DNA. Sometimes people are adopted into a family, sometimes family members are related through marriage, and sometimes we have people that we choose to consider part of our families. My nieces are my husband's sister's daughters—we aren't related by blood, but I absolutely love being their Aunt Kara. Two of my cousins were adopted, but they and their children help to carry on many of the traditions of our family. It doesn't matter that we don't share DNA; we share love, family celebrations, holidays, and more stories than I can count. I also have friends in my life who I consider a part of my chosen family—these are the people who we know will be there when needed, no matter what.

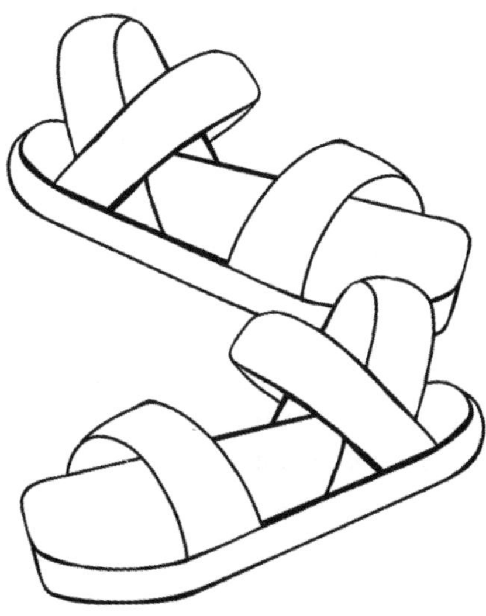

In today's story, we meet two women named Ruth and Naomi. Naomi and her husband moved to Moab because of a food shortage at home, and Naomi gave birth to two sons in Moab. Ruth and Naomi became family members when Ruth married Naomi's son Mahlon. Sadly, Naomi's husband and both of her sons die. But after Mahlon died, Ruth chose to still consider Naomi (her mother-in-law) a part of her family. When Naomi decided to return to her original home, Ruth had the option of going back to her parents' home, but she decided she would rather remain with Naomi.

In Ruth's time, there were no cars or highways, trains or airplanes. Some people might have had a donkey to ride, and the very wealthy might have access to a horse, but the average person simply had to walk from one location to another. In fact, historians tell us that at that time, most people never traveled farther than ten miles from where they were born. This means that Ruth knew she would most likely never see her home or her family again, if she chose to travel with Naomi. Ruth deciding to go with Naomi was a very big deal.

Ruth decided that Naomi was her family and that she even wanted to follow the same God that Naomi worshiped. Even though there had been so much sadness in their family, they found comfort in the small family they had left. Ruth was demonstrating Lilo's modern mantra about family: "No one gets left behind or forgotten."

Ruth and Naomi walked all the way back to Naomi's original home, on dusty roads with only sandals as footwear. After arriving in Bethlehem (the town that many years later became Jesus' birthplace), Ruth eventually married again, and she and her husband had children. One of their children became an ancestor of Jesus! God has designed us to be in community with each other, and part of our community consists of our family, whatever shape that family might take.

We are studying many stories from the Bible this Advent while we wait for Christmas. There are a lot of stories that come from our families that help make up who we are. In the same way, Jesus' life was influenced by the stories of the family members who had come before him, like his ancestor Ruth. But the story of God's people doesn't end with Jesus—you are also a part of God's ongoing story in the world. How can your current family be a part of God's ongoing love in the world?

Reflection Questions

1. Today's symbol is a pair of sandals. Why is this the symbol for today? What does it mean?

2. Who are the people you consider family? Are there people whom you love who aren't related to you by DNA? Who are they?

3. Ask your grown-ups to tell you some familiar locations that are more than ten miles away from your home. What would it be like if you had never traveled farther than that? Would it be scary to go so far?

4. What does family mean to you? God gives us an important gift in giving us family, as God often works through people who love us. How do we honor God by treasuring the gift of family?

Repeat-after-Me Prayer

This is a repeat-after-me prayer!

Dear God,
we give you thanks
for all the people
whom we call family.
Be with our family members.
Watch over them and care for them.
Help us to love them
as much as you love us.
In Jesus' name we pray,
Amen.

THIRD WEEK OF ADVENT

Shiphrah, Puah, Jochebed, and Miriam
Exodus 1:8–2:25

A special note for grown-ups: Today's devotion includes some difficult topics, including slavery, death, and even murder. These are difficult topics but still incredibly relevant to our world today. A lot of these are topics that children sometimes encounter far younger than we may deem "appropriate." It is possible to have these difficult conversations with kids while also assuring them that they are safe and loved. It's possible to name these difficult topics and then let kids guide our conversations with their own questions and curiosity.

Today we have a really exciting story about four superheroes! A long time ago, there were two women named Shiphrah and Puah who worked as midwives in Egypt. A midwife is a person who helps a mother give birth to a new baby. At that time, the Israelites were enslaved in Egypt, and the pharaoh (who was like a king) became afraid of how strong the Israelites had become. Pharaoh was so afraid that he did a horrible thing:

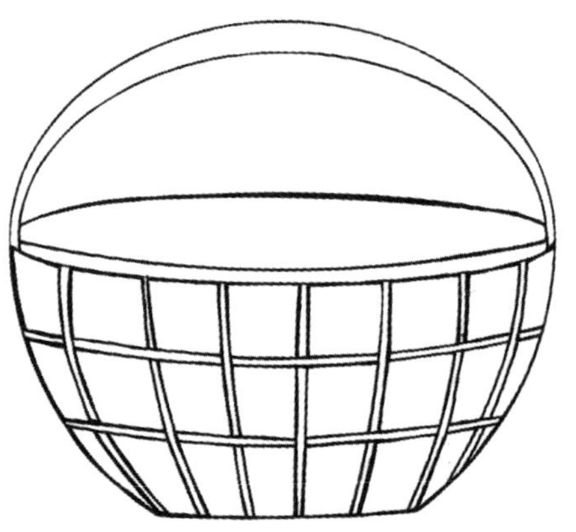

he ordered the midwives Shiphrah and Puah to murder boy babies as they were being born. Both women knew this was wrong, so they refused to do what Pharaoh had ordered them to do. They could have been horribly punished for not following Pharaoh's orders, but they were more concerned with making the right choice.

When Pharaoh realized there were still boys being born to the Israelite people, he did another horrible thing. He ordered his soldiers to throw all baby boys under the age of two into the Nile River. A woman named Jochebed decided to keep her baby, Moses, safe from this terrible fate, and she hid her new baby for as long as she was able. Eventually she knew she couldn't hide him anymore, so she wove a special basket that would float and placed him in the basket on the Nile River. Moses' sister Miriam followed the basket along the riverbank to see where it wound up.

Eventually, an Egyptian princess, daughter of the pharaoh himself, found the basket with the baby, Moses. She decided that she would adopt the baby from the basket and raise him as her own son. After Moses grows up, God calls him to lead the Israelite people out of slavery and into the land God promised.

We see a lot of people who are referred to as superheroes in our TV shows, movies, comic books, and video games. A lot of times these superheroes are depicted as very muscular and strong. But in our Scripture today, we read about four women who are superheroes because their actions save their own people. Shiphrah, Puah, Jochebed, and Miriam may not have looked like superheroes on the outside, but God made all of them brave and filled them with courage to do the right things. Just like those four women so long ago, God can also fill us with courage and strength to make good choices and treat other people with kindness, even when it's the hard thing to do.

We are getting closer and closer to Christmas, which is another part of God's greater ongoing story. When Jesus was born, there were a lot of bad things going on in the world around him—including a ruler who was just as mean as the pharaoh had been. Just like baby Moses had to be hidden to be kept safe, baby Jesus had to be hidden to keep him safe—his parents traveled all the way to another country to protect him. Jesus has a lot of nicknames, and one of them is Emmanuel, which literally means "God with us." We are excited as we continue to wait for Christmas, and it is a joy to know that God is always with us, even when we are called to do what is difficult.

Reflection Questions

1. Today's symbol is a basket. Why is this the symbol for today? What does it mean?

2. Name some superheroes that you know from TV, movies, comic books, video games, etc.

3. Now name some people in your life who you know love you and help keep you safe. How are these people you know in real life similar to superheroes from stories? How might you grow up to become a superhero in someone else's story?

4. Sometimes making the right choices can be difficult. How can God help you to choose what is kind and what is loving in your life?

Repeat-after-Me Prayer

This is a repeat-after-me prayer!

Dear God,
we give you thanks
for people who look ordinary
but are really superheroes for you!
Help us to remember
that you can be at work within us
to choose what is loving
and what is kind.
Help us to turn to you
when we are challenged
with making the right choices!
In Jesus' name we pray.
Amen.

FOURTH SUNDAY OF ADVENT

Magnificat
Luke 1:46–56

Today's Scripture passage has a strange title; people who study the Bible refer to it as the Magnificat. This is from a Latin word that means "my soul magnifies," which is a phrase taken directly from Mary's words in our Scripture reading for today. Our souls are an invisible force within us that make us who we are. "My soul magnifies God" may seem like strange words, but I bet you already know what *magnify* means. Do you know what a magnifying glass does? It makes objects bigger and clearer, and it can make light more concentrated. In our Scripture today, Mary is saying that her soul (her heart and mind) is like a magnifying glass for God! She wants God to shine through her life; she wants her life to help people see God more clearly.

Through Mary's Magnificat, she talks about what God is going to do through her baby Jesus when he grows up. Mary says that Jesus is going to create change on earth and will work to make life better for people who don't have very much say in the world. Throughout Jesus' teaching and ministry, he frequently sides with people who feel left out or ignored, and in our Scripture passage, Mary is predicting that Jesus will do this during his life.

Our symbol for today is a dove, usually depicted in this context as a white bird. This is used in the Christian tradition as both a symbol for the Holy Spirit as well as a symbol of peace. Mary is filled with God's Holy Spirit when she speaks the words we read today. She is proclaiming that Jesus' coming into the world will mean a new peace for the souls of God's people.

Reflection Questions

1. Today's symbol is a dove. Why is this the symbol for today? What does it mean?

2. Talk with your grown-ups about what makes them feel at peace.

3. After your grown-ups share what makes them feel at peace, consider what makes you feel at peace—both in your body and in your soul. What would the world be like if more people felt at peace inside themselves?

4. Have you ever felt left out or ignored? It probably wasn't a nice feeling. Since God frequently sticks up for the people who feel left out or ignored throughout the Bible, how do you think God wants us to treat those people when we encounter them?

Repeat-after-Me Prayer

This is a repeat-after-me prayer!

Dear God,
we give you thanks
that you sent Jesus into the world
to stand up for people
who often feel left out or ignored.
Help us to remember
what it feels like to be left out
and to do our best
in showing other people
how much we love them

and how much you love us all.
In Jesus' name we pray.
Amen.

CHRISTMAS EVE

Jesus Born in Bethlehem
Luke 2:1–7

We know that Christmas Eve is one of the most exciting nights of the year because tomorrow, when we wake up, it will be Christmas morning! You might even be putting out some cookies and milk tonight to prepare for Santa Claus to visit. But it's important to remember, as Christians, that Christmas isn't just about the presents, getting time off school, and all the delicious food that comes with the holiday season. Today we remember that we are celebrating something so much bigger. We are celebrating God, the Creator, coming to live among us in the person of Jesus.

As humans, God created us to live in community with one another. We are made to thrive when we are close to the people we love. Have you ever felt as if you needed to be near someone, maybe a parent, a friend, or a sibling? Have you ever been far apart from someone you loved and wanted desperately to see them? God wanted to be with us so much that God was willing to become human to spend time with us.

My younger sister, Kelli, drew all the pictures for this book. Even though I was only three years old when Kelli was born, I very clearly remember meeting my younger sister for the first time. My grandparents took me to see her, and I remember my dad helping me wash my hands several times, and then I put on a special, clean gown before I was allowed to go into the room to see my mom and the baby. While some people may choose to give birth at home, the majority of people alive today in the United States were born in hospitals. But there is no hospital in our Scripture story today. Why not?

First, in Jesus' time, they didn't have hospitals like we have today. There might have been a gathering place where a healer could tend to multiple patients at the same time, but there wasn't a specific location where you went if you were sick or in need of a doctor. In those days, frequently there were women known as midwives who helped mothers give birth, but they usually came to visit the mothers' homes.

Second, Mary and Joseph are far from home. The Roman government had forced them to travel, even though Mary was close to giving birth. The Scripture says that Mary laid Jesus in a manger, which is a long trough from which animals (like donkeys and cattle) eat hay. Mary gave birth to Jesus next to the spot where the owners of the house fed their farm animals. This was not a sterilized and clean environment, like a hospital room. People visiting didn't have a special hand-washing station and didn't put on clean gowns to come into the room. This was a very messy way for Jesus to come into the world.

But this is part of how we know that God loves us so much. God isn't afraid of the dirt or the mess—God wanted to become human and live with us. It was so important that God didn't care how dirty or gross things might be on earth—God still wanted to be with us.

Reflection Questions

1. Today's symbol is a manger. Why is this the symbol for today? What does it mean?

2. Name a time when you have missed another person. Why did you want to be close to them? How did you feel when you finally got to see that person?

3. God created us to live in community with one another. Have your grown-ups help you name all the communities you are a part of. Consider how much you are loved in those communities. God loves us just as much!

4. What is the real meaning of Christmas for Christian people? Whose birth are we celebrating today and tomorrow? Why does that matter?

Repeat-after-Me Prayer

This is a repeat-after-me prayer!

Dear God,
we are so excited
for Christmas to finally arrive.
Help us to remember
that we are celebrating
how much you love us,
and we are celebrating
that you came into the world
to walk with us.
As we celebrate with friends and family
and consider how we are surrounded by love,
help us to remember your love for us!
In Jesus' name we pray.
Amen.

CHRISTMAS DAY

Shepherds Visit Jesus
Luke 2:8–20

While there are many farmers in our modern world, shepherds are pretty rare. When Jesus was born, being a shepherd was a fairly common profession. A shepherd is a person who watches over a flock of sheep all the time. Unlike modern ranches, ancient grazing grounds for livestock weren't surrounded by fences. The livestock needed to be moved daily from one place to another to get enough grass. To accomplish this, and to keep them safe, shepherds actually lived out in the fields with their sheep. When nighttime came, they laid down on the ground and went to sleep with their flocks in the field. Shepherds had to fend off both thieves and an abundance of predator animals that roamed that part of the ancient world, which included lions, bears, leopards, hyenas, wolves, and jackals. And often the only tools they had to fight off these predators were a slingshot and a shepherd's staff. (A shepherd's staff looks like a human-sized candy cane.) Imagine fighting off a lion with a big stick!

Shepherds had to be very brave, but because they lived in the fields with their sheep, they were not very clean. Imagine how dirty you would get if you went camping for a few weeks with no access to a shower or a bath. Your skin would get pretty grimy, and you might not smell very nice. Because this was how the shepherds lived, they were dirty and didn't smell very pleasant.

And yet these are the first people that God invites to come meet the baby Jesus. An angel appears to the shepherds in the fields and invites them to come to see Jesus in the animal trough where Mary and Joseph have set him to sleep. God could have come into the world to the richest people on earth and been placed in an expensive bassinet with a gold rattle in each hand. God could have invited queens and kings drenched in expensive perfumes to be the first people to see the incarnate Divine. Instead, this humble beginning is what God chose. God wanted to experience what it was like to be an ordinary human being, so God embraced all the messiness that is a part of being human.

It was important to God that people knew Jesus was for everyone. Jesus didn't come for just the special, talented, or wealthy. Jesus came for all people, including all children, all over the world. God made sure that ordinary people were invited to the birth of Jesus, because God loves ordinary people just the way we are. Jesus came for people just like us so that we could all be a part of God's greater story, and God made sure that the world understood that.

Reflection Questions

1. Today's symbol is a sheep. Why is this the symbol for today? What does it mean?

2. Human bodies can get very dirty—from dirt, mud, paint, food, and all sorts of other things. Name a time when you were playing and got really messy. Do you think that a mom would have been happy to have you come see her newborn baby while you were like that? Or do you think your grown-ups would ask you to clean up first? Why does God invite shepherds, who are pretty messy, to be the first people to meet Jesus?

3. Pretend you are going to throw a party, and have your grown-ups help you make a list of who you would invite.

Why are these people on the list? What does it mean that when God throws a party, everyone is invited?

4. Name a time when you were very afraid. What was it like, and how did it feel? Why do you think the shepherds were afraid when they saw the angel? How can the angels' words help speak to us when we are afraid?

Repeat-after-Me Prayer

This is a repeat-after-me prayer!

Dear God,
we give you thanks
that you loved us so much
you wanted to be with us
and were born as a human
through the baby Jesus.
Help us to remember
how much you love us,
but also help us to remember
how much you love all people.
Everyone we ever meet
is created in your divine image
and loved by you.
Thank you for the love we experience
through the story of Christmas!
In Jesus' name we pray.
Amen.

SUNDAY AFTER CHRISTMAS

Zechariah and Elizabeth
Luke 1:5–17

How do grown-ups know when they receive a message? When they get a phone call, text message, or email, how do they know that someone is trying to communicate? Most likely, they receive some sort of notification—either a sound, ringtone, or a buzzing alert—that lets them know someone is trying to get in touch.

In today's Scripture passage, we read about Zechariah and Elizabeth, who learned that they were going to have a baby and God wanted them to name him John. They found out about John because Zechariah had a vision of an angel—a messenger of God—who told him that Elizabeth was expecting a baby. At first, Zechariah didn't believe the good news and thought it was too good to be true.

John's birth was special because Zechariah and Elizabeth believed they couldn't have children, and so they were both excited to learn that they were going to have a baby. John's birth was extra special because an angel came to visit to tell Zechariah about the life John would lead. John was one of Jesus' cousins and was just a few months older than Jesus. John was chosen to be a messenger who prepared people to hear from Jesus. In the ancient world, no one had cell phones or computers. They had to spread messages by word of mouth, by sending another person with their message, or by writing down the message on a piece of parchment. God asked John to help spread the story about Jesus before Jesus even started his teaching and ministry.

When I receive exciting news, I want to share it with everyone in my life. I want all my friends and family to know that something wonderful has taken place. You probably feel the same way when you receive good news—like you might burst if you have to keep the information to yourself. You want to share your good news with the world! God felt the same way and sent John into the world to proclaim to anyone who would listen that Jesus had arrived—to be on the lookout for the good news Jesus would share. God had a story to share with the world, and John's ministry made sure people were ready to receive that story of good news.

Reflection Questions

1. Today's symbol is an angel. Why is this the symbol for today? What does it mean?

2. Ask a grown-up to tell you about ways to communicate that they remember from their childhood. Did they ever receive letters or invitations by mail? Did they have a landline for their phone? How did people spread the word about something exciting before social media and text messages? (If your grown-ups are too young to remember these things, find some older grown-ups to ask.)

3. When you receive good news, how do you feel? How do you share your good news with other people?

4. Why did God want to tell the world about Jesus? What was John's role in how God told the world about Jesus' story?

Repeat-after-Me-Prayer

This is a repeat-after-me prayer!

Dear God,
we give you thanks
for all the ways
you communicate with us.
Thank you for Scripture,
and for all the people
who teach us about you.
Help us to open our hearts
to receive your message
and give us courage to share

the good news of your love.
In Jesus' name we pray.
Amen.

WEEK AFTER CHRISTMAS

Jesus Presented at the Temple
Luke 2:22–24

The birth of a new baby brings about a lot of change for the rest of the family in the household. Even though a new baby can be wonderful and exciting, change isn't always easy. First-time parents are learning how to do a lot that they have never done before. But even when experienced parents are welcoming a new baby, there are changes in the lives of the family members. New babies aren't yet able to do anything for themselves, and this means that they need constant care and attention. Sometimes they need a lot of attention in the middle of the night, so people caring for the baby are exhausted. Siblings of new babies experience a lot of changes at home as well.

Mary and Joseph were only a few days into all these new changes when their religious beliefs required that they take baby Jesus to the temple. Even though people who follow Jesus are called Christians, Jesus himself was Jewish. This was because Jesus' earthly parents, Joseph and Mary, also practiced a religion called Judaism. There are still people who practice Judaism in our world today. A long time ago, when Jesus was born, Jewish parents brought their sons to the temple in Jerusalem when they were eight days old. At the temple, the entire family participated in certain religious ceremonies.

Even though this was a special day for Mary and Joseph, it would have been a fairly ordinary day for the people at the temple; eight-day-old babies were brought in all the time. But Jesus wasn't an ordinary baby. This is why both Simeon and Anna begin to speak about how important Jesus is to the world and how he will do amazing things when he grows up.

Both Simeon and Anna begin to speak with prophecy—which means that God gives them guidance to speak about what will happen in the future. Simeon is very old, and he is excited that he has seen the hope that Jesus represents before he dies. He speaks of how Jesus will be the one to save the people of Israel. At that time in history, the people of Israel were under something called occupation from the Roman Empire. This meant that Israelites didn't have the full rights that other citizens had and could be treated very unfairly by the Roman government that was in charge. Simeon is excited that Jesus represents God doing something new among the people of Israel. Simeon talks about how Jesus will serve as a light to help people see God more clearly.

Simeon is using light as a metaphor to speak, once again, about the hope that people can find in God. There is hope that when this baby grows up, he might help the people to be set free from the Romans. There is hope that Jesus will be the person they have been waiting for who will lead them into a future where they no longer need to be afraid.

The prophet Anna speaks about how Jesus will bring about redemption for Israel, a fancy way of saying Jesus will save the people from evil. Anna has waited her whole life for this moment, and she is so excited that she got the chance to meet Jesus.

Even though an ordinary baby changes a lot of things for an entire family, both Anna and Simeon were excited because they knew that when baby Jesus grew up, he would create change for all the people of the world. We remember and celebrate that change through the good news of Christmas.

Reflection Questions

1. Today's symbol is a candle. Why is this the symbol for today? What does it mean? In a world without electricity, how do you think candles were used?

2. Ask your grown-ups to tell you some stories about when you joined the family. What changes happened in their home when you joined the household. What was it like for your grown-ups? What changed in their lives?

3. What does it mean that Anna and Simeon were prophets who spoke prophecy?

4. Name a time when you thought you were being treated unfairly. What happened, and what was it like? How did you feel? What do you think it feels like for groups of people when an entire government or culture treats them differently from other people?

Repeat-after-Me Prayer

This is a repeat-after-me prayer!

Dear God,
we give you thanks
for all the ways
you speak through us.
Help us to make sure
that other people
are treated with fairness
and kindness in the world.
Help us to stand up
when someone is being mistreated,
and remind all your people
that God loves everyone!
In Jesus' name we pray.
Amen.

JANUARY 6 (EPIPHANY)

Journey of the Magi
Matthew 2:1–15

You probably know what gold is—a precious metal. In both the modern and ancient worlds, it was used to produce expensive jewelry and coins, and in the modern world it is sometimes used in industrial production. Part of the reason humans have found it so valuable is that it is easy to shape and does not react very much with other chemicals, so it stays shiny and keeps its color. But what are frankincense and myrrh?

The other two gifts the magi bring are both made from dried tree sap, sap being the sticky liquid that lives inside of trees. If you've ever had maple syrup on pancakes or waffles, you've already eaten a version of tree sap before, in its liquid form. Unlike liquid maple syrup, frankincense and myrrh are harvested and dried-out tree sap, but just like maple syrup, frankincense and myrrh have very distinct smells. In the ancient world, this good-smelling stuff was given a lot of value, meaning it was incredibly expensive to purchase. This means that only someone with a lot of money could afford to buy gold, frankincense, and myrrh.

These may seem like strange gifts to give to a baby. If you've ever been to a baby shower, the parents-to-be probably did not put these three items on their baby registry; people were probably giving the new parents things like diapers, bottles, cribs, and the other things people need to care for babies in modern times. But because these gifts carried so much value in the ancient world, these were the sort of presents that magi would bring to someone in a royal family; these were gifts fit for a king.

During the Christmas season, it is common to give Christmas gifts to people we love and to receive gifts as well. One of the reasons we practice this tradition is to celebrate the gifts that the magi brought to Jesus and to remember that Jesus is a gift that God gave to the entire world.

We don't know how many magi there were. Even though nativity scenes frequently depict three magi, the Scripture just tells us there are more than two. The tradition of three magi in Western culture comes from the three gifts that are named in Scripture. Interestingly, in some Christian cultures, the magi are depicted with twelve people instead of three. Even though we don't know how many there were, they were incredibly important to Jesus' story. They came from a long way away (most likely traveling by camel) and are important because they represent that Jesus came for the entire world, not just for people in one small area. This is because God loves humans so much, God wanted that love to be available to everyone, not just one small group. And that good news of God's love is why we celebrate Christmas together as Christan people!

Reflection Questions

1. Today's symbol is a camel. Why is this the symbol for today? What does it mean?

2. What gift were you most excited to receive this past Christmas? What were the gifts the magi brought for baby Jesus, and why did they bring those presents?

3. Have your grown-ups help you make a list of some items that are important to take care of a new baby. Ask your grown-ups to tell you about gifts that people have given them to help out with raising you.

4. Name a time when you felt left out. What happened? How did it feel? Why do you think it was important for God to let the whole world know that Jesus was for everyone and that no one would be left out of God's love?

Repeat-after-Me Prayer

This is a repeat-after-me prayer!

Dear God,
we give you thanks
that Jesus came
for all the people of the world.
Help us to welcome other people
as you have welcomed us
and to love other people
as you have loved us.
Help us to make sure people
feel included at school and church,
within our teams and groups,
and in our love.
We thank you
for the gift of Jesus,
who came into this world
because you love us so much!
In Jesus' name we pray.
Amen.

Acknowledgments

There are so many people who helped make this book possible. Thank you to my sister, Kelli Cooper. I am grateful for all your beautiful illustrations that helped bring this book to life. I am also grateful for all the encouragement you give me in my writing endeavors. I hold tight to the advice you once gave me when I told you I didn't know how to do something: "Then learn." Those are words to live by. Thank you for editing the first round of this project.

For Chris Cooper, my fantastic brother-in-law—thank you for your words of support and for encouraging Kelli as she worked on the illustrations for this book. Thank you for keeping all our houses in working order and generously sharing your knowledge and time.

To Ken and Wanda Eidson, my parents, for all their ongoing support. I am grateful for the faith foundation you provided me and thankful for all the ways you continue to offer encouragement. Thank you for the fond childhood memories I have of doing our Jesse tree readings together as a family during Advent. Thank you for editing the first round of this book.

Thank you to Revs. Blair Zant, Allison Marcus, and Melissa Gepford. I am grateful to you for offering your insights, knowledge, expertise, and experience to the reflections in this book.

I am grateful to my childhood pastor, Rev. Adam Hamilton. Thank you for the support you have given me across the years when I answered my call to ministry as well as encouraging me to pursue my dreams of becoming a published author.

Rev. Paul Smith, you always encouraged me to ask difficult questions and to never shy away from difficult answers. I am thankful for the stories you taught me and the ways you taught me to craft a story.

Thank you to my professors from Duke Divinity. I am grateful for the foundation of your teaching. To my Duke Divinity friends Blair, Jenn, and Sarah: as always, your friendship continues to be a balm to my soul. I can't wait to see how our stories progress. I am grateful for your support across the miles and across the years.

To the congregations of McLouth United Methodist Church and Oskaloosa United Methodist Church: thank you! I know how fortunate I am to be your pastor, and I am grateful for all of you. Thank you for inviting me in and allowing me to be a part of the stories of your communities.

Thank you to the team at Westminster John Knox Press, especially Jessica Miller Kelley, Natalie Smith, and the marketing team. I am grateful for your patience, guidance, and wisdom in the process of creating this new book.

And finally, to my amazing husband, Michael Lee. I am forever grateful for your ongoing support and encouragement and for your belief in my abilities. I love you very much, and I can't believe how fortunate I am that we get to live this amazing story together!

Notes

1. Mary Doria Russel, *The Sparrow* (Ballantine Books, 1996), 201.

2. *Dr. Who,* episode 213, "A Christmas Carol," written by Steven Moffat, aired December 25, 2010, on BBC One.

3. Victor H. Matthews, *Social World of the Hebrew Prophets* (Hendrickson, 2001), 27.

4. Sara Groves, "Generations," *Conversations,* INO Records, 2001.

5. Buddy Greene and Mark Lowry, "Mary, Did You Know?" *Michael English,* Warner Alliance Records, 1991.

6. Lewis R. Donelson, "Christmas Day: John 1:1–14," in *Feasting on the Word: Preaching the Common Revised Lectionary, Year B, Volume 1,* ed. David L Bartlett and Barbara Brown Taylor (Westminster John Knox Press, 2008), 143.

7. *Lilo and Stitch,* directed by Chris Sanders and Dean DeBlois, (Walt Disney Pictures, 2002).

8. *Lilo and Stitch.*